Hudson History
of Settle

PEDIGREE OF THE GAWTHORPE SHUTTLEWORTHS.

Henry de Shuttleworth
of Shuttleworth Hall
= Agnes – dau and heiress of William
de Hacking of Hacking Hall

Ughtred de Shuttleworth
of Gawthorpe (living 1388)

Hugh Shuttleworth
(living 1463)

Lawrence Shuttleworth
(living 1527)
= Elizabeth Worsley – dau of Richard Worsley
of Mearley and Twiston.

Nicholas Shuttleworth
(living 1527)
= Ellen – dau of Christopher Parker
of Radholme Park, Yorks.

Hugh Shuttleworth
(1504 – 96)
= Anne – dau of Thomas Grimshaw
of Clayton Hall. d. 1597
m. 1540

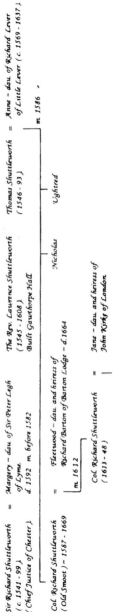

Sir Richard Shuttleworth
(c. 1541 - 99)
(Chief Justice of Chester)
= Margery – dau of Sir Peter Legh
of Lyme.
d. 1592 m. before 1582

The Rev. Lawrence Shuttleworth
(1545 - 1608)
Built Gawthorpe Hall

Thomas Shuttleworth
(1546 - 93)
= Anne – dau of Richard Lever
of Little Lever (c. 1569 - 1637)
m. 1586

Nicholas

Ughtred

Col Richard Shuttleworth
(Old Smoot) – 1587 - 1669
= Fleetwood – dau and heiress of
Richard Barton of Barton Lodge – d. 1664
m. 1612

Col Richard Shuttleworth
(1613 - 48)
= Jane – dau and heiress of
John Kirke of London.

Richard Shuttleworth (of Forcet) – 1644 - 81. = m. 1664 Margaret – dau. of John Tempest d. 1683

Sir Richard Shuttleworth 1666 - 87. = m. 1682 Catherine – dau. and heiress of Henry Clarke – Magdalen College – Oxon 1667 - 1728

Richard Shuttleworth 1683 - 1749 – (Ready Money Dick) = m. 1707 Emma – dau. of William Tempest – d. 1725

James Shuttleworth 1714 - 73. = m. 1742 Mary – dau. and heiress of Robert Holden of Aston Hall – Derbyshire – 1718 - 91.

Richard – 1708 - c1730. d. unmarried in Naples.

Robert Shuttleworth c 1745 - 1816. = m. 1776 Anne – dau. of Gen. Thomas Desgauliers d. 1801.

Robert Shuttleworth – c 1784 - 1818. "The People's Magistrate" – inherited Gawthorpe = m. 1816 Janet – dau. of Sir John Marjoribanks d. 1855

James Shuttleworth of Barton – d. 1846. (inherited Barton)

Janet Shuttleworth heiress – 1817 - 72. = m. 1842 Sir James Kay-Shuttleworth – 1st Baronet 1849 1804 - 77 (became Kay-Shuttleworth 1842)

Sir Ughtred Kay-Shuttleworth – 2nd Bt. (1844 - 1939) – created Lord Shuttleworth 1902. = m. 1871 Blanche – dau. of Sir Woodbine Parish 1851 - 1924

Angela 1872 - 1967

Nina 1879 - 1948

Rachel 1886 - 1967

Flying Officer Richard, 2nd Lord – 1913 - 40 – Killed in action

Capt. Lawrence 1887 - 1917 Killed in action = m. 1913 Selina – dau. of Gen. Francis Bridgeman

Capt. Ronald 3rd Lord 1917 - 42 – Killed in action

Capt. Edward – 1890 - 1917 Killed on military service = m. 1914 Sibell – dau. of Charles Adeane of Cambridge.

Catherine 1894 - 1963

Major Charles 4th Lord – 1917 - 75 Gave Gawthorpe to Nat. Trust, 1970 = m. 1947 Anne – dau. of Col. Phillips

Charles – 5th Lord b. 1948 = m. 1975 Anne – dau. of James Whatman

©   Michael P. Conroy   2003

Published by:- Hudson History Procter House, Kirkgate.

Settle. N.Yorks. BD24 9DZ. Tel 01729 825773

I.S.B.N.   1-903783-18-6

Printed by:- LPD, Station Road, Settle. N.Yorks

Previous Publications:-

      Backcloth To Gawthorpe. First Edition.   1971

                          Second Impression.   1979

                     Revised & Enlarged. 1996

     The Shuttleworths of Gawthorpe.   1999

Title Page Illustration:- Gawthorpe Hall in 1966.

MYSTERIES AND MEMORABILIA OF GAWTHORPE AND THE SHUTTLEWORTHS

CHURCHES CONNECTED
WITH THE SHUTTLEWORTHS
AT THEIR VARIOUS ESTATES

BARBON MANOR

FORCETT HALL

LECK HALL

> ✠
> St. Bartholomew's
> Barbon

KIRKBY LONSDALE

> ✠
> St.Cuthbert's
> Forcett

RICHMOND

> ✠
> St. Peter's
> Leck

BARTON ESTATE

GAWTHORPE HALL

> ✠
> St. Anne's
> Woodplumpton

PRESTON

> ✠
> St. Leonard's
> Padiham

PADIHAM

> ✠
> All Saints
> Habergham

BURNLEY

This Plan is not drawn to scale.

MYSTERIES AND MEMORABILIA OF GAWTHORPE AND THE SHUTTLEWORTHS

CONTENTS

LORD SHUTTLEWORTH,
THE PRESENT LORD LIEUTENANT OF LANCASHIRE

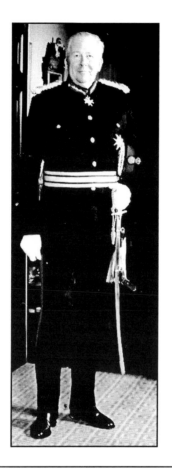

CHARLES GEOFFREY NICHOLAS,
THE FIFTH BARON SHUTTLEWORTH

Lord Shuttleworth resides at Leck Hall, Lancashire.

FOREWORD
BY THE FIFTH LORD SHUTTLEWORTH

Michael Conroy knows a great deal more than I do about my family, to his credit and perhaps to my shame, and he has compiled an invaluable source of reference which is in constant use by me. It is work like his which makes many today realise the interest that lies in our ancestry, and in knowing where we come from. I am particularly lucky that in learning about my forebears, I find that most of the research has been done for me by the author of this fascinating work. I hope others will find as much intriguing information as I do in these pages.

SHUTTLEWORTH

THE FAMILY OF THE FIFTH LORD SHUTTLEWORTH

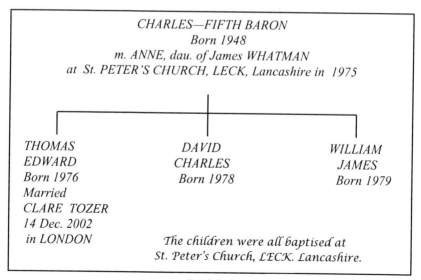

CHARLES—FIFTH BARON
Born 1948
m. ANNE, dau. of James WHATMAN
at St. PETER'S CHURCH, LECK, Lancashire in 1975

THOMAS
EDWARD
Born 1976
Married
CLARE TOZER
14 Dec. 2002
in LONDON

DAVID
CHARLES
Born 1978

WILLIAM
JAMES
Born 1979

The children were all baptised at
St. Peter's Church, LECK. Lancashire.

PREFACE

This third book of the series on the Shuttleworths of Gawthorpe is the result of various requests for information from Local Historians regarding unexplained and confusing puzzles connected with Gawthorpe Hall which is situated between Burnley and Padiham in N.E. Lancashire. These problems were originally broached as a series of articles entitled 'Mysteries of Gawthorpe' which I was asked to write for the 'Lancashire History Quarterly'.

Family Historians also request details of the Memorials connected with the Shuttleworth family and their servants. I have included all that I could find, some in a poor condition, others, unfortunately already lost. Information of any others will be gratefully received. There are examples from Padiham, Altham and Habergham in Burnley, Mitton near Whalley, Walmersley near Bury, Bamford near Rochdale, Broughton and Woodplumpton near Preston, Barbon near Kirkby Lonsdale, and Forcett, north of Richmond in North Yorkshire together with Orsett in Essex and Brompton Cemetery, London. There are also a number of inscriptions from the Lancashire area together with Civil War correspondence and items from Prince Edward Island, Canada and Grays, Essex relating to Robert Shuttleworth. I have included the wills of Thomas and the two Robert Shuttleworths as a further source of information.

I am grateful to Lord Shuttleworth for his helpful suggestions, photographs and kind words in the foreword of this publication. I also thank the Chetham Society for permission to quote from their publications and to the Bolton and District Family History Society for the Will of Thomas Shuttleworth, together with Ron Smith for his unstinting help. I am also grateful for the assistance given by the staffs of Burnley, Bolton, Bury, Kendal, Ramsbottom, Richmond, Rochdale, Skipton and York Reference Libraries, the Borthwick Institute, York, Cumbria Record Office, Lancashire Record Office, the Harris Library, Preston, Manchester Central Library, Towneley Hall and Gawthorpe Hall.

I am indebted to the Vicars of the churches concerned who gave their permission to photograph the Memorials and quote the Parish Registers: Rev. Chris. Cousins of Altham, Rev. David Wiseman of Bamford, Rev. Richard Mitchell of Barbon, Rev. David Jenkins of Broughton, Rev. Quentin Harcourt Wilson of Burnley, Rev. Mike L. Hartley of Colne & Villages, Rev. Stanley Haworth of Forcett, Rev Alan Morris of Greenmount, Rev. Chris. Rogers of Habergham, Rev. John Birbeck Of Mitton, Rev.Vanessa G. Cato of Orsett, Rev. James Watson of Woodplumpton, and to the Churchwardens of Padiham, John Sellick and Mitton, Peter Lancaster for their invaluable assistance. Mr. James Heathcote of Forcett Hall was also most helpful as was Christine Anderson of Forcett St. Cuthbert's, Doris Crossley of Altham St. James and Jill Cragg of Downham St. Leonard's. I am grateful, too, for the valuable help given by Terry Carney of Grays Thurrock Museum , the Essex Family History Society and Boyde Beck of Prince Edward Island Museum, Canada, together with Diane Waters, secretary of the L.F.H.H.S. London branch.

I owe the fine layout of the Pedigree on the inside covers to Steve Howarth of the Lancashire Family History Computer Section and the details from the Protestation Oaths to Tony Foster, Chairman of the Lancashire Family History Society. I also wish to thank David Francis and John & Elizabeth Benson for their meticulously drawn illustrations. I am indebted to Michael Geraghty for the detailed photographs and information on Orsett St. Giles together with Judith Church. I am also most grateful for the excellent photographs of the London graves supplied by Frank Ashworth and Keith Duerden. I have quoted from Roger Fulford's notes on the Shuttleworth family and David Webber's 'Robert Shuttleworth, the Opulent Gentleman from Morell' together with the reminiscences of John Harrison on the Gawthorpe Estate.

Susan Bourne and Mike Townend have been most accommodating regarding references to the Towneley archives and John & Maureen Hartley have greatly assisted me with wills. Ken Spencer and Margaret Jones have kindly supplied invaluable items of information from their vast knowledge of the Burnley and Padiham areas and archives. Lyn Hartley, I.T. Consultant, could not have been more helpful and Anne Conroy, as always, has given valuable help with typing. I am indebted to Molly Haines, the Chairman of Burnley Historical Society, for meticulously proof-reading the manuscript. My grateful thanks to all who have aided my research and apologies to anyone I have inadvertently omitted. Finally I owe a huge debt of gratitude to Margaret, my long suffering wife, for accompanying and sustaining me on my journeys and for her forbearance and invaluable advice during the extended research for the trilogy.

GAWTHORPE WAS FIRST OCCUPIED
BY UGHTRED SHUTTLEWORTH IN 1389
AND RETAINED BY THE FAMILY UNTIL 1970

Gawthorpe is situated between Burnley and Padiham in North East Lancashire, on the A671 just off the M65.

Ughtred Shuttleworth first rented land there in 1389 during the period when John of Gaunt was Duke of Lancaster and Lord of the Manor of Ightenhill. The Shuttleworths prospered by judicious marriages and land acquisitions so that by the late 1500s an affluent descendant of Ughtred's, Sir Richard Shuttleworth, Chief Justice of Chester, together with his younger brother and agent, Thomas, was able to aquire the estates of Barbon in Lancashire and Forcett in Yorkshire. Richard also drew up the plans for the erection of Gawthorpe Hall before his untimely death in 1599.

Gawthorpe Hall

Richard's brother, the Rev. Lawrence Shuttleworth brought these plans to fruition in the years 1600 - 1604 and on his death in 1608 the Estate was inherited by Richard (later Colonel), the son of his younger brother Thomas who had pre-deceased both of his elder brothers Sir Richard and the Rev. Lawrence in 1593. The Barton estate came with the marriage of Richard (later Colonel) Shuttleworth to Fleetwood Barton in 1612.

The Shuttleworths held Gawthorpe until 1970 when the Fourth Lord Shuttleworth gave it to the National Trust.

MYSTERIES

SINCE THE FIRST UGHTRED SHUTTLEWORTH OF GAWTHORPE RENTED LAND THERE IN 1389 THERE HAVE BEEN A NUMBER OF ITEMS CONNECTED WITH THE ESTATE AND THE HALL THE EXPLANATION FOR WHICH IS UNKNOWN. PERHAPS AT SOME FUTURE DATE THESE MYSTERIES WILL BE SOLVED.

THE MYSTERY OF

THE ANCIENT PARCHMENT

This ancient parchment regarding Ughtred, the first Shuttleworth of Gawthorpe, was written in the early 15th. century, in English with the dialect of East Lancashire. It was found by the Author in the old Estate Office at Gawthorpe. Translated into modern English it reads:-

'Gracious and discreet Lord, John Parker of Ightenhill accuses Ughtred of Shuttleworth at the King's suit in the hall-mote of Ightenhill that he did not come with his corn that grew at Gawthorpe where he lives to Burnley mill. And the aforesaid Ughtred gave answer that the aforesaid place was under no obligation to come to Burnley mill, and never did these last 40 years for it has been his that length of time, nor had he ever heard tell from old men, or in writings that the aforesaid corn should come thither. The land in question is custom-land and the

corn from it goes to the King's mill of Padiham and he pays as other customers
do, so the King incurs no loss from this. Praying you that I might continue to do
as the aforesaid place has been seized in the time of all lords and all stewards.
John Parker of Ightenhill says he has paid a fee before Roger Flour, formerly
chief steward, for a place of land that is called Royle, that has never been subject
to such fee before, which is a great loss to the king; praying you for the
advantage of the king that I might have a copy of the record of his fee; and I
shall give you a deed of the aforesaid land as law and custom requires, and I will
say no more, when you tell me to desist.'

What was the result of Ughtred's plea? Was he allowed to continue to send his corn to Padiham Mill? Padiham mill was much nearer but obviously not under the stewardship of John Parker, unlike Burnley, and Parker hoped for the 'socage' or dues from Ughtred's crop. We do know that the Shuttleworths later held both Padiham and Burnley Corn Mills from the early seventeenth century into the twentieth century.

Did the first Shuttleworth of Gawthorpe obtain a copy of the fee paid by John Parker for Royle? Royle was on the east side of Ightenhill and had 40 acres of land, meadow and wood together with a fishpond for the manor house. Did Ughtred have prior claim to Royle with a deed he offered to give, presumably claiming his right to the place? Whatever the outcome, John Parker was described as being 'of Royle' in 1423 and it was leased to John Parker in 1425. However, the Shuttleworths did gain a foothold in Royle in the mid seventeenth century when Margaret Shuttleworth was married to Nicholas Towneley of Royle.

The ancient parchment still holds some of its secrets.

THE MYSTERY
OF THE DATE
ON THE WOODEN TABLET

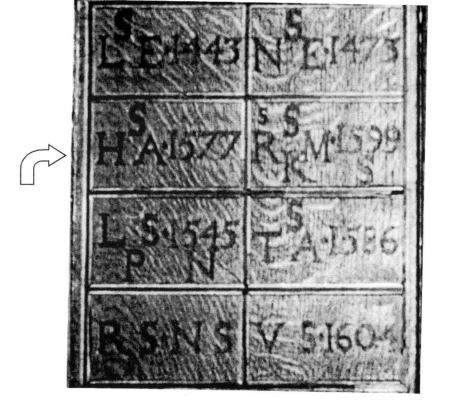

Gawthorpe is the ancestral seat of the 5th. Lord Shuttleworth, the Lord Lieutenant of Lancashire. The initials of a number of his earliest ancestors are to be found on a wooden tablet originally erected in 1604 which is now situated in the entrance hall.

This interesting old wooden tablet was originally above the fireplace in the Wainscot Room above. This room was demolished in 1850 to give extra height to the entrance hall.

On the panels are a series of dates giving the birth, marriage or death of the Shuttleworth in that panel. The exception is the date 1577. Hugh Shuttleworth was born in 1504, he was married in 1540 and he died in 1596. His wife Anne died the following year, 1597. What then could be the significance of 1577?

Perhaps the answer lies with the person who erected the tablet. This was the son of Hugh, Lawrence, 'Mr. Parson Shuttleworth' the Rector of Whichford, a man of puritanical views. This can be shown by the plaster rose he had placed on the ceiling of the room in which the tablet was placed, which read 'God Save Us From Turk And Pope'. 1577, the date in question, was the year of the first Census of Papists (which was the basis of the 1579 laws which imposed fines on recusants).

Hugh had been born and married before the Reformation and was probably still able to attend Mass until 1573 for Padiham Church appears to have had a Catholic priest until that date. By this time, being in his seventieth year, he would be reluctant to change his ways. His sons doubtless thought otherwise. The prospect of fines would not appeal to son Thomas, the accountant for the estate. Similarly the prospect of forthcoming restrictions on holding office, probably known to the eldest son, Judge Richard, might affect that son's prospects, too if it were known that his father was a papist. Lawrence with his strong puritan convictions could well have provided the final straw that determined Hugh to accept the Reformed Church in 1577 before the census deadline. Hence this date would be very important to Lawrence, his father's 'new birth date'- when he was 'born again'!

LAWRENCE
'MR. PARSON
SHUTTLEWORTH'

PAGE 11

THE MYSTERY OF
THE INITIALS ON THE
DRAWING ROOM FIREPLACE

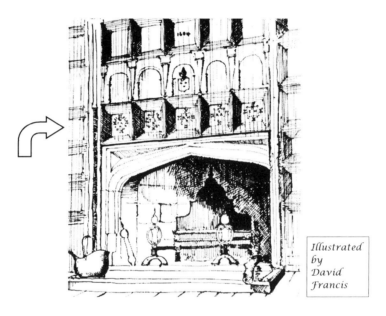

Illustrated
by
David
Francis

Five wooden panels with initials were incorporated in the overmantle of the

Drawing Room at Gawthorpe in 1604.

S	S	S		
W	H	S	S	O
T A	T I	R M	R A	E M
K	K	K		
1	*2*	*3*	*4*	*5*

THE EFFIGY OF
SIR RICHARD
SHUTTLEWORTH

THE EFFIGY OF
MARGARET
SHUTTLEWORTH

The initials in panel 3 are those of Sir Richard Shuttleworth of Gawthorpe and his wife Margaret. (The effigies of this couple can be seen above the fireplace.) The remaining four panels are those of their important relatives.

Panel 2 is that of Sir Thomas Halsall and his wife Jane, who was the sister of Sir Richard's grandmother Margaret (nee Stanley), whilst panel 5 is that of their daughter, Matilda and her husband Edmund Osbaldeston.

Panel 1 has the initials of Sir Thomas Walmesley and his wife Anne, nee Shuttleworth, the heiress of Hacking Hall. It is panel 4 which is the mystery panel. Various historians have proffered their views. Bishop Shuttleworth in his pedigree stated that Sir Richard's uncle Richard succeeded to Hacking and was the father of Anne in the first panel and it is his and his wife Anne's initials. The Rev. T. D. Whitaker, on the other hand said, in 1806, that the heiresses parents were Robert and Jane.

To confuse matters still further John Harland in 1856 maintained that the initials were those of Robert Shuttleworth and his wife Anne (nee Desaguliers) who were married in 1776! This would imply that panel 4 was placed in position later, perhaps to replace a damaged square.

Bishop Shuttleworth's explanation appears to be the most logical as it fits the pattern of the squares i.e. parents and their children, but the initials R, S and A remain one of the Gawthorpe mysteries.

PAGE 13

THE MYSTERY OF

THE MISSING MULLET

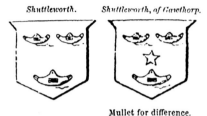

Shuttleworth.   Shuttleworth, of Gawthorp.

Mullet for difference.

*The above diagrams are from
'Gregson's Portfolio of Fragments'.*

Illustrated by David Francis

On the overmantle in the 'Lords' (Huntroyde) room at Gawthorpe Hall can be seen

the Coat of Arms of the Gawthorpe Shuttleworths in plasterwork (above, left). It

contains the same shield as that over the entrance doorway erected when the Hall

was built in 1600-4. The mystery is that up to 1594, at least, the Shuttleworths had a

Mullet (or Star) in the Fesse Point or centre of the shield (see small diagram above,

right.). This was the same shield as that held by the Shuttleworths of Hacking Hall as

both families were descended from Henry, a third son of Henry de Shuttleworth of

Shuttleworth Hall, Hapton. His father, also called Henry, had been granted the

shield with three shuttles (above, centre) in 1329.

As there have not been any Shuttleworths of Shuttleworth Hall since the

late 1300s (the heiress having married John de Legh), or at Hacking Hall since he

late 1500s, (the heiress having married Judge Walmesley) it appears that the

Gawthorpe Shuttleworths, now being the premier family, have decided to dispense

with the Mullet.

THE MYSTERY
OF THE
BARTON SHIELDS

BARTON OF	BARTON OF
SMITHILLS	**BARTON**

Shields by the late Jock Shaw of the Lancashire Heraldry Group.

There were two Barton heiresses who married into the Shuttleworth family.

Margaret Barton of Smithills Hall, near Bolton, Lancashire married Sir Richard

Shuttleworth and Fleetwood Barton of Barton Lodge, near Preston, Lancashire

married Colonel Richard Shuttleworth. They are both depicted on carved

shields above the entrance to the Long Gallery at Gawthorpe Hall. Both these

carvings carry the same shield, the Three Boars Heads of Barton as in the right

hand diagram above, yet the Bartons of Smithills carried as their shield the

Three Harts Heads, as in the above left hand diagram. Was this a careless

mistake on the part of woodcarvers inexperienced in the carving of shields (note

the lack of hatching to denote colours) or was there some other reason?

THE MYSTERY
OF THE
SHIELD ON THE BED

Illustrated by Elizabeth Benson

On the bedhead of this old Gawthorpe bed is a shield incorporating the coats of arms of C olonel R ichard S huttleworth and his bride F leetwood B arton. H er arms are not the arms they used on their Family Tree, the three Boars of Barton, but for some mysterious reason she used the six martlets of Fleetwood. Was this a fanciful whim of the young bride, Fleetwood, who had just changed her surname from Barton to Shuttleworth or was there some deeper meaning?

THE MYSTERY
OF
THE HOARD OF GOLD COINS

Illustrated by David Francis

During the restoration of the Hall by Sir Charles Barry in 1850 a mysterious hoard of 39 Portugese gold coins and 52 English guineas was found under a window seat in the Wainscot Room when this room was being demolished to give extra height to the entrance hall. There were no coins dated later than 1745, the time when the Hall was under the stewardship of the Nowells who were a Royalist family. The Shuttleworths at this time were living on their estate at Forcett, in Yorkshire.

The person who secreted them must have been a Jacobite and it has been suggested that Frances Towneley, a friend of the Nowells, may have been housed at Gawthorpe prior to meeting Bonnie Prince Charlie in Manchester at the end of 1745. He was later taken prisoner at Carlisle and beheaded in London at Tyburn in 1748, his head being set on a pike above Temple Bar. (This head was kept for years in the chapel at Towneley Hall until it was interred in the family vault in St. Peter's church, Burnley in 1947). Could he have hidden the coins before his departure, his unfortunate death prior to his planned return accounting for the coins remaining at Gawthorpe?

MEMORIALS

THE FOLLOWING SELECTIONS OF MEMORIALS WERE IN THE VARIOUS CHURCHES CONNECTED WITH THE SHUTTLEWORTH ESTATES, ALTHOUGH A NUMBER HAVE BEEN MOVED FROM THEIR ORIGINAL SITE. SOME ARE NOW IN A POOR CONDITION, OR HAVE DISAPPEARED ALTOGETHER.

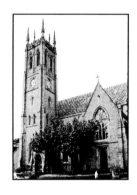 

Padiham St. Leonard's   *Habergham All Saints*

Barbon St. Bartholomew's   *Forcett. St. Cuthbert's*

Padiham St. Leonard's church is situated in the centre of the town whilst Habergham All Saints is on the edge of the Gawthorpe estate.
Barbon St. Bartholomew's is in the village of the same name in Cumbria, north of Kirkby Lonsdale, whilst Forcett St. Cuthbert's is in the village of Forcett, north of Richmond in Yorkshire.

PAGE 18

MEMORIAL TO THOMAS YATES
(SERVANT TO COLONEL RICHARD SHUTTLEWORTH)
ON THE SOUTH WALL IN PADIHAM PARISH CHURCH 1643

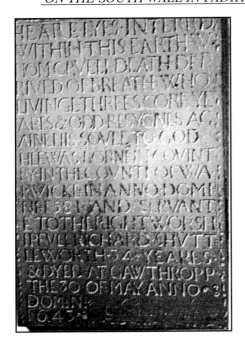

IT SAYS:-

HEARE LYES INTERRD
WITHIN THIS EARTH W
HOM CRUELL DEATH DEP
RIVED OF BREATH WHO
LIVING THREE SCORE YE
ARES & ODD RESYGNES AG
AINE HIS SOULE TO GOD
HEE WAS BORNE IN COVINT
RY IN THE COUNTI OF WAR
WICKE IN ANNO DOMI
NI 1581 AND SERVANT
E TO THE RIGHT WORSH
IPFULL RICHARD SHUTT
LEWORTH 34 YEARES
& DYED AT GAWTHROPP
THE 30 OF MAY ANNO
DOMINI
1643   *Thomas Yates*

*Thomas Yates duties included
making periodic visits on
horseback to London, York,
Manchester, Stourbridge and
Wigan to deal with
business for the Gawthorpe Estate.*

WHICH READS:-

*HEARE LYES INTERRD WITHIN THIS EARTH
WHOM CRUELL DEATH DEPRIVED OF BREATH
WHO LIVING THREE SCORE YEARES & ODD
RESYGNES AGAINE HIS SOULE TO GOD
HEE WAS BORNE IN COVINTRY IN THE COUNTI
OF WARWICKE IN ANNO DOMINI 1581 AND
SERVANTE TO THE RIGHT WORSHIPFULL
RICHARD SHUTTLEWORTH 34 YEARES & DYED
AT GAWTHROPP THE 30 OF MAY ANNO DOMINI
1643*

Thomas Yates

COLONEL
RICHARD
SHUTTLEWORTH

TOMBSTONE OF THE SECOND
SIR RICHARD SHUTTLEWORTH (1666-1687)
IN PADIHAM PARISH CHURCH 1687

IT READS:-

S RICHARD SHVTTLEWORTH. DYED
THE 27th. OF JVLY 1687.

This simple stone was originally in the central aisle near the communion rails before it was moved to the side altar during the period when the church floor was tiled.

Above the name was a shield, now completely worn away , bearing:-

ARMS:- In the first and fourth quarters :-
the three shuttles for SHUTTLEWORTH
In the second and third quarters :-
the three boars for BARTON.

Sir Richard died at Gawthorpe when he was twenty-one years of age.
He left a wife, Catherine, aged twenty, and three children.

MEMORIAL TABLET TO
ROBERT SHUTTLEWORTH (1784-1818)
AT ONE TIME SITUATED ON THE NORTH WALL
IN PADIHAM PARISH CHURCH 1818

"Sacred to the memory of

ROBERT SHUTTLEWORTH Esq.

of Gawthorpe Hall.

He departed this life, deeply lamented,

on the 6th. day of March, in the year

of our Lord, 1818,

And in the 32nd. year of his age.

His remains are interred under the pew

belonging to the family in this church."

The ARMS on this tablet were, Per Pale;
Dexter;   SHUTTLEWORTH Quartering BARTON;
Sinister;   Argent, on a chief, gules, a cushion,
Between two spur rowels of the field,
for MARJORIBANKS.

This Monument was described in 1856 as
'A mural tablet, by S. Joseph, of Edinburgh',
and was placed on the north wall,
surmounted by a funereal urn.

What happened to it subsequently is unknown.

WHITE MARBLE MEMORIAL TO
JANET KAY-SHUTTLEWORTH (1817-1872)
ON THE SOUTH WALL IN PADIHAM CHURCH 1872

 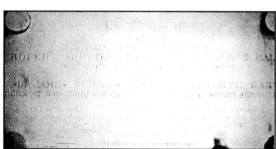

As this memorial is on white marble and the letters are not picked out, the inscription is difficult to see.

IT READS:-

IN MEMORY OF
JANET
ONLY CHILD OF THE LATE
ROBERT SHUTTLEWORTH OF GAWTHORPE HALL
IN THE COUNTY OF LANCASHIRE, ESQUIRE
WIFE OF
SIR JAMES PHILLIPS KAY-SHUTTLEWORTH BART.
BORN AT GAWTHORPE HALL NOV. 9 1817.
DIED AT SODEN SEPT. 14 1872.

O DEATH WHERE IS THY STING O GRAVE WHERE IS THY VICTORY
THE STING OF DEATH IS SIN   AND THE STRENGTH OF SIN IS THE LAW
BUT THANKS BE TO GOD WHICH GIVEST US THE VICTORY

MORS VIA AD VITAM

Janet was buried in Bad Soden,
east of Frankfurt, Germany, on Sept. 16th. 1872.

BRASS MEMORIAL PLAQUE FOR
SIR JAMES KAY-SHUTTLEWORTH (1804-1877)
ON THE SOUTH WALL IN PADIHAM CHURCH 1877

IT READS:-

IN MEMORY OF
SIR JAMES PHILLIPS KAY-SHUTTLEWORTH BART. D.C.L.
OF GAWTHORPE HALL AND BARBON MANOR.
BORN JULY 20th. 1804:   DIED MAY 26th. 1877.
HE WAS SECRETARY TO THE COMMITTEE
OF COUNCIL ON EDUCATION FROM ITS
FORMATION IN 1839 TO 1849:   HIGH SHERIFF OF LANCASHIRE IN 1864:
VICE CHAIRMAN OF THE FUND FOR THE RELIEF OF DISTRESS OF THE
MANUFACTURING DISTRICTS 1862 TO 1865.

"THE WORK OF OUR HANDS ESTABLISH THOU IT"
"TO HIM THAT SOWETH RIGHTEOUSNESS SHALL BE A SURE REWARD"
"THEY REST FROM THEIR LABOUR AND THEIR WORKS DO FOLLOW THEM"

James was buried in Brompton Cemetery, (East Position, Compartment 5.)
Fulham Road, London. SW10 9UG, on 29th. May 1877.

For the life of Sir James Kay-Shuttleworth read
'Journey of an Outsider' by R. J. W. Selleck
and 'The Life and Work of Sir James Kay-Shuttleworth' by Frank Smith.

PAGE 23

HATCHMENT INSTALLED
IN ALL SAINTS CHURCH, HABERGHAM
FOR JANET KAY-SHUTTLEWORTH
ON HER DEATH IN 1872

This hatchment is in need of restoration.

ARMS:- Quarterly: first and fourth, SHUTTLEWORTH,
(with canton), second and third, KAY.
Centre chief:- Badge of Ulster.

Small shield (In pretence):-
Arms:- Quarterly: first and fourth, SHUTTLEWORTH,
second and third, BARTON.
Crests:- First, SHUTTLEWORTH. Second, KAY.

Motto of KAY:- Kynde Kynn Knawne Kepe
(Kind friends know and keep.)

Funeral Hatchments came into vogue in the 17c. but are rarely used today.
They were usually carried at the funeral procession and then were erected on
the wall of the church after the funeral service. The word 'hatchment' is a
corruption of 'achievement' (a display of the person's armorial devices).

It was Janet's vision to build a church next to the school that she had
erected in Habergham on the perimeter of the Gawthorpe Estate. She
achieved this in cooperation with the Dugdales of Lowerhouse in 1846.

MEMORIAL WINDOW TO
ALFRED FORD,
GAWTHORPE AGENT,
IN HABERGHAM CHURCH 1913

DETAIL:-

THE FULL INSCRIPTION READS :-

TO THE GLORY OF GOD AND IN
MEMORY OF
ALFRED FORD,
AGENT TO THE
GAWTHORPE ESTATE
FOR MORE THAN FORTY YEARS AND FORMER
OFFICER OF THIS **CHURCH** WHO DIED
OCTOBER 8th. 1913.
THIS WINDOW WAS GIVEN BY HIS FRIENDS.

Besides the upkeep of the Hall and grounds, Mr. Ford had to supervise the forestry, mining, roads, housing and farming relating to the estates. The latter included dairy farming at Gawthorpe, sheep at Barbon and cheese, eggs and pigs at Inskip.

MEMORIAL TO CHARLES CAMM

THE SHUTTLEWORTH'S COACHMAN.

IN HABERGHAM CHURCH 1924

IT READS:-

IN MEMORY OF CHARLES CAMM
B. 16 DEC. 1856 — D.AUG. 1924
FOR 34 YEARS, FROM 1890, HE
WAS THE TRUSTY COACHMAN
OF LORD & LADY SHUTTLEWORTH
OF GAWTHORPE.
"WELL DONE, GOOD & FAITHFUL SERVANT"

LORD
UGHTRED
SHUTTLEWORTH

LADY
BLANCHE
SHUTTLEWORTH

Charles Camm, the coachman, always said that he would serve Lady Shuttleworth as long as she lived and in fact died two months after she did in 1924.

MEMORIAL TO BLANCHE MARION,
LADY SHUTTLEWORTH (1851-1924)
IN HABERGHAM CHURCH   1924

IT READS:-

THE CLOCK
WAS PLACED IN THE TOWER
BY THE PARISHIONERS OF
HABERGHAM IN AFFECTIONATE
REMEMBRANCE OF THEIR
FRIEND AND NEIGHBOUR
BLANCHE MARION WIFE OF
LORD SHUTTLEWORTH
OF GAWTHORPE + 1924

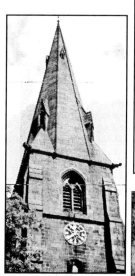

*Lady Shuttleworth was buried
in the family plot at Barbon
Church where she had laid the
foundation stone in 1892.
(See Pages 29 and 31)*

PAGE 27

THE SHUTTLEWORTHS
HAVE HELD THE BARBON ESTATE
NEAR KIRKBY LONSDALE SINCE THE 1590s.

Barbon estate was bought by
Sir Richard Shuttleworth in the 1590s.

Barbon Manor

In 1863 Sir James Kay-Shuttleworth built the Manor on the side of the valley at Barbon as a hunting lodge for his sons. It was originally intended as the 'shooting box'. After his wife Janet died in 1872, his eldest son Ughtred inherited Gawthorpe together with the other Shuttleworth estates and James resided at Barbon prior to his death in 1877. (He had been staying with his daughter in San Remo when his health deteriorated and he was rushed to hospital in London where he died.) He was buried in Brompton Cemetery on the 29th. Of May 1877 near to his London home at 68, Cromwell Rd., South Kensington. The Barbon Estate continued to be administered by the Shuttleworths who used it for sheep farming and grouse shooting. The fifth Lord Shuttleworth's grandmother Sibell lived at the manor with her third husband Sir Roger Fulford until her death in 1980. (See P. 45).

FOUNDATION SHIELD

OF ST. BARTHOLOMEW'S

CHURCH, BARBON 1892

Lady Shuttleworth had laid the foundation stone for
the church on the 19th. April 1892. There is a brass
plate in the sanctuary (shown above) inscribed:-

To the Glory of GOD.
———
This stone was laid
on Easter Tuesday
1892
by Blanche Marion,
Lady Kay-Shuttleworth.

+

PAGE 29

WEST WINDOW OF St. BARTHOLOMEW'S CHURCH,
BARBON, PRESENTED BY
BLANCHE , LADY SHUTTLEWORTH 1893

 DETAIL:-

THE FULL INSCRIPTION READS:-

'THIS WINDOW IS DEDICATED TO LOUISA, WIFE OF
SIR WOODBINE PARISH K. C. H.* BY HER DAUGHTER
BLANCHE M. KAY SHUTTLEWORTH. A.D. 1893'

*Knight Commander of Hanover.
Sir Woodbine Parish was the last English survivor of this title.

MEMORIAL TO
1st. LORD & LADY SHUTTLEWORTH
IN BARBON CHURCH   1939

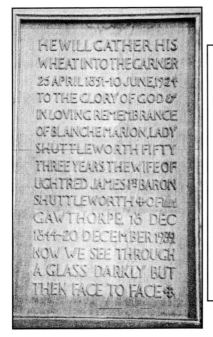

IT READS:-

HE WILL GATHER HIS
WHEAT INTO THE GARNER
25 APRIL 1851-10 JUNE 1924
TO THE GLORY OF GOD &
IN LOVING REMEMBRANCE
OF BLANCHE MARION LADY
SHUTTLEWORTH FIFTY
THREE YEARS THE WIFE OF
UGHTRED JAMES BARON
SHUTTLEWORTH OF
GAWTHORPE. 18 DEC
1844-20 DECEMBER 1939
NOW WE SEE THROUGH
A GLASS DARKLY BUT
THEN FACE TO FACE +

*Lord Shuttleworth lived at Barbon Manor in his old age
and died there, aged 95, on 20th. December 1939*

PAGE 31

MEMORIAL TO THE MEN OF BARBON
WHO FELL IN THE FIRST GREAT WAR.
REMEMBERED IN BARBON CHURCH 1919

LAWRENCE
KAY-
SHUTTLEWORTH

EDWARD
KAY-
SHUTTLEWORTH

IT READS:-

1914 + 1919
TO THE HONOURED MEMORY
OF THE MEN OF
THE PARISH OF BARBON
WHO FELL IN THE GREAT WAR

THOMAS ARTHUR AIRLY
EDWARD BOND
WILLIAM BOND
WILLIAM JAMES SHARP
LAWRENCE U. KAY SHUTTLEWORTH
EDWARD J. KAY SHUTTLEWORTH
WILLIAM HENRY TALLON

BY THEIR SACRIFICE WE LIVE

THE KAY-SHUTTLEWORTH
BURIAL PLOT
IN BARBON CHURCHYARD

A NUMBER OF THE KAY-SHUTTLEWORTH FAMILY ARE INTERRED HERE, FROM THE FIRST LORD SHUTTLEWORTH ONWARDS. THE INSCRIPTIONS ON A NUMBER OF THE GRAVESTONES ARE ALMOST ILLEGIBLE AND WILL SHORTLY BE INDECIPHERABLE.

Details of the inscriptions on the War Memorial Cross are to be found on Pages 36 & 37 and on the double Page 38/39

GRAVE OF EDWARD KAY-SHUTTLEWORTH (1890-1917)
(FATHER OF THE 4th. LORD SHUTTLEWORTH)
IN BARBON CHURCHYARD 1917

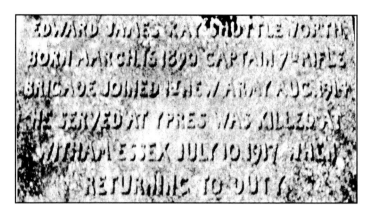

IT READS:-

EDWARD JAMES KAY-SHUTTLEWORTH
BORN MARCH 16th. 1890 CAPTAIN 7th. RIFLE
BRIGADE JOINED 1st. NEW ARMY AUG. 1914
HE SERVED AT YPRES. WAS KILLED AT
WITHAM ESSEX JULY 10 1917 WHEN
RETURNING TO DUTY.

Note:-
Edward had been home on leave
to see his newborn son
(who later became the
4th. Lord Shuttleworth)

GRAVE OF THE FIRST
LORD AND LADY SHUTTLEWORTH
IN BARBON CHURCHYARD   1939

DETAIL:-

IT READS:-

LORD SHUTTLEWORTH
18th. DEC 1844 - 20 DEC. 1939
LORD LIEUTENANT OF LANCASHIRE
1908 -1928

HE WILL GATHER HIS WHEAT
INTO THE GARNER

BLANCHE MARION
53 YEARS THE WIFE OF
UGHTRED JAMES LORD SHUTTLEWORTH
10th. JUNE 1924

PUT THOU THY TRUST IN THE LORD

NAMES ON THE BASE OF THE
SHUTTLEWORTH WAR MEMORIAL CROSS
IN BARBON CHURCHYARD 1947

MAJOR COLERIDGE EUSTACE HILLS
R.A.S.C.
(SON OF NINA KAY-SHUTTLEWORTH AND EUSTACE HILLS)

LIEUT. EDWARD DEREK WALTER LEAF
R.N.V.R. D.S.C. and BAR
(SON OF CATHERINE KAY-SHUTTLEWORTH AND LIEUT. CHARLES LEAF)

CHARLES SYMONDS LEAF.
E. KENT REG. MGC. RAF., R. MARINES 1895 – 1947
(HUSBAND OF CATHERINE KAY-SHUTTLEWORTH)

LIEUT. JOHN ANTHONY LYTTELTON
GRENADIER GUARDS
(SON OF SIBELL, WIDOW OF EDWARD KAY-SHUTTLEWORTH)

SURGEON COMMANDER DOUGLAS A. NEWBERY
ROYAL NAVY
(SON IN LAW OF ANGELA KAY-SHUTTLEWORTH)

MAJOR THE HON. SIR THOMAS W. A. FRANKLAND
BART. 15/19 HUSSARS
(SECOND HUSBAND OF PAMELA K-S, DAUGHTER OF EDWARD KAY-SHUTTLEWORTH)

THE BASE ALSO INCLUDES THE TWO LORD SHUTTLEWORTHS OPPOSITE.
PAGE 36

SECTION OF THE WAR MEMORIAL CROSS DEDICATED
TO THE 2nd. & 3rd. LORD SHUTTLEWORTHS
IN BARBON CHURCHYARD 1947

RICHARD UGHTRED PAUL	RONALD ORLANDO LAWRENCE
K.S. BART.	K.S. BART.
2nd. BARON SHUTTLEWORTH	3rd. BARON SHUTTLEWORTH

These were the two sons of Lawrence Kay-Shuttleworth, the eldest son of Ughtred, the first Lord Shuttleworth. Lawrence had died in the first World War. Richard inherited on the death of Ughtred in 1939 but he was killed in the Battle of Britain in 1940 leaving his younger brother Ronald as his heir but he, too, was killed in action, in 1942 in North Africa.

THE KAY-SHUTTLEWORTH FAMILY

UGHTRED JAMES KAY-SHUTTLEWORTH 1844 ——

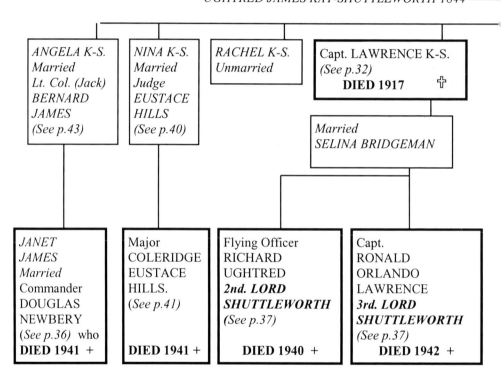

ANGELA K-S. *Married* *Lt. Col. (Jack)* *BERNARD* *JAMES* *(See p.43)*	*NINA K-S.* *Married* *Judge* *EUSTACE* *HILLS* *(See p.40)*	*RACHEL K-S.* *Unmarried*	Capt. LAWRENCE K-S. *(See p.32)* **DIED 1917** ✠ *Married* *SELINA BRIDGEMAN*

JANET JAMES *Married* Commander DOUGLAS NEWBERY *(See p.36)* who **DIED 1941 +**	Major COLERIDGE EUSTACE HILLS. *(See p.41)* **DIED 1941 +**	Flying Officer RICHARD UGHTRED ***2nd. LORD*** ***SHUTTLEWORTH*** *(See p.37)* **DIED 1940 +**	Capt. RONALD ORLANDO LAWRENCE ***3rd. LORD*** ***SHUTTLEWORTH*** *(See p.37)* **DIED 1942 +**

✠ **ON THE 1914-1919 WAR MEMORIAL**
IN BARBON CHURCH

(SEE MEMORIAL ON PAGE 32)

LOSSES IN THE TWO WORLD WARS

*—— 1939 1st. **LORD SHUTTLEWORTH***

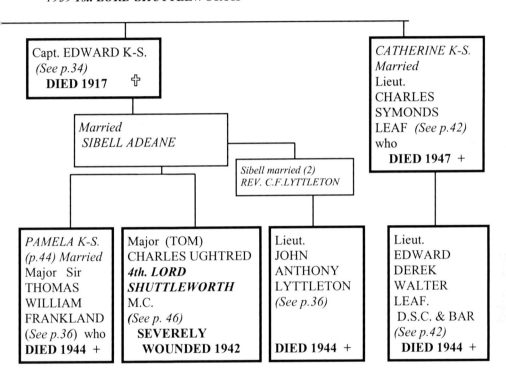

Capt. EDWARD K-S.
(See p.34)
DIED 1917 ✠

Married
SIBELL ADEANE

*Sibell married (2)
REV. C.F.LYTTLETON*

*CATHERINE K-S.
Married
Lieut.
CHARLES
SYMONDS
LEAF* *(See p.42)*
who
DIED 1947 +

*PAMELA K-S.
(p.44) Married
Major Sir
THOMAS
WILLIAM
FRANKLAND
(See p.36)* who
DIED 1944 +

Major (TOM)
CHARLES UGHTRED
***4th. LORD
SHUTTLEWORTH***
M.C.
(See p. 46)
**SEVERELY
WOUNDED 1942**

Lieut.
JOHN
ANTHONY
LYTTLETON
(See p.36)
DIED 1944 +

Lieut.
EDWARD
DEREK
WALTER
LEAF.
D.S.C. & BAR
(See p.42)
DIED 1944 +

**+ ON THE SHUTTLEWORTH CROSS
IN BARBON CHURCHYARD**

(SEE DETAILS OF THE CROSS ON PAGES 36/37)

MEMORIAL TO NINA, DAUGHTER OF
THE 1st. LORD SHUTTLEWORTH
IN BARBON CHURCHYARD 1948

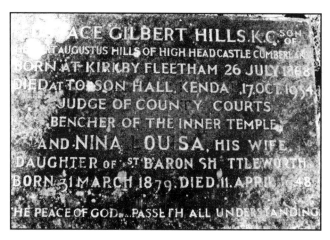

IT READS:-

EUSTACE GILBERT HILLS K.C. SON OF
HERBERT AUGUSTUS HILLS OF HIGHHEAD CASTLE CUMBERLAND
BORN AT KIRKBY FLEETHAM 26 JULY 1868
DIED AT TOLSON HALL KENDAL 17 OCT. 1934
JUDGE OF COUNTY COURTS
BENCHER OF THE INNER TEMPLE
AND NINA LOUISA, HIS WIFE
DAUGHTER OF 1st. BARON SHUTTLEWORTH
BORN 31 MARCH 1879. DIED 11 APRIL 1948

THE PEACE OF GOD PASSETH ALL UNDERSTANDING

Nina wrote 'The Life of Sir Woodbine Parish' and was co-authoress
with her sister Angela, of the book, 'The Life of Mrs. John Brown'.

MEMORIALS TO THE CHILDREN OF
NINA (née K-S.) & EUSTACE HILLS
IN BARBON CHURCHYARD 1922-1941

IT READS:-

IT READS:-

JOHN MICHAEL UGHTRED
BELOVED SECOND SON OF
EUSTACE HILLS K.C.
AND NINA HIS WIFE
BORN 1st. SEPT 1915
DIED 1st. AUG 1922
HE TooK A LITTLE CHILD & BLESSED HIM

MAJOR C.E. HILLS
ROYAL ARMY SERVICE CORPS.
17th. DECEMBER 1941
AGED 29
BORN 3rd. AUGUST 1912

*John Michael Hills and Coleridge Eustace Hills were two of
the grandsons of the first Lord Shuttleworth.*

MEMORIAL TO CATHERINE,
THE YOUNGEST DAUGHTER OF
THE 1st. LORD SHUTTLEWORTH,
TOGETHER WITH HER HUSBAND AND SON
IN BARBON CHURCHYARD 1963

THE LORD IS MY SHEPHERD
THEREFORE I WILL FEAR NAUGHT

CATHERINE
BLANCHE LEAF
BORN 7th. APRIL 1894
DIED 18th. OCT 1963

BELOVED WIFE OF
CHARLES
SYMONDS LEAF

IT READS:-

BURIED AT BROOKWOOD

✠

LIEUTENANT E. D. W. LEAF
D.S.C. & BAR B.A. F.R.G.S.
ROYAL NAVAL VOL. RESERVE
15th. FEB 1944
AGE 25
ALSO HIS WIFE
DOREEN LAURIE
4th. AUG.1995 aged 76

IT READS:-

*Lieutenant Edward Derek Walter Leaf was
another grandson of the first Lord Shuttleworth.*

MEMORIAL TO ANGELA MARY,
THE ELDEST DAUGHTER OF
THE 1st. LORD SHUTTLEWORTH,
TOGETHER WITH HER HUSBAND
IN BARBON CHURCHYARD 1967

 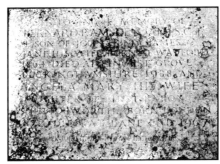 

IT READS:-

IN LOVING MEMORY OF
BERNARD RAMSDEN JAMES: COL.
4th. SON OF
JOHN HENRY JAMES & JANE HIS WIFE.
BORN AT WATFORD 1864
DIED AT FINGEST GROVE,
BUCKINGHAMSHIRE 1938
AND
ANGELA MARY
HIS WIFE
DAUGHTER OF FIRST BARON
SHUTTLEWORTH
BORN LONDON 1872
DIED AT LANE END 1967

AMONG THE VERY BRAVE THE VERY TRUE

For the life of Angela James read 'A Very Remarkable Woman'
By Pennie Denton.

GRAVESTONE OF PAMELA, SISTER OF
THE 4th. LORD SHUTTLEWORTH
IN BARBON CHURCHYARD 1972

IT READS:-

PAMELA MABELL CATHERINE
PARDOE
BORN 17. 9. 1915   DIED 15. 9. 1972
WIFE OF
ROBERT HUGH PARDOE
BORN 22. 2. 1914   DIED 21. 6. 1975
DAUGHTER OF
EDWARD & SIBELL KAY-SHUTTLEWORTH

The second husband of Pamela Kay-Shuttleworth, Major Sir
Thomas Frankland, died in 1944, his name is on the
Shuttleworth War Memorial at Barbon. (See pages 36 and 39).
The memorial to her son by the Hon. William Keith Rous,
her first husband (son of the Earl of Stradbroke), is on page 49.
He was Lieutenant General Sir William Rous K.C.B., O.B.E.

GRAVESTONE OF
SIBELL & SIR ROGER FULFORD
IN BARBON CHURCHYARD 1983

IT READS:-

SIBELL   ELEANOR
MAUD   FULFORD
1890-1980
WIFE OF
ROGER   FULFORD
Kt C V O
1902 - 1983

Sibell was the widow of Edward Kay-Shuttleworth. (See P. 34)
Sibell and Edward were the parents of Pamela K-S (P.44)
and Charles Ughtred, the 4th. Lord Shuttleworth. (P. 46/47)
Sir Roger, Sibell's third husband, received a Knighthood for services to the Liberal Party
and a CVO for his work on the histories of various Members of the Royal Family.

PAGE 45

GRAVESTONE OF THE
4th. LORD SHUTTLEWORTH (1917-1975)
IN BARBON CHURCHYARD 1975

IT READS:-

TOM
CHARLES UGHTRED
JOHN 4th. BARON
SHUTTLEWORTH M.C.
of GAWTHORPE
24th. JUNE 1917
5th. OCTOBER 1975

The 4th. Lord Shuttleworth was known by the name of 'TOM'.

MEMORIAL TO
4th. LORD SHUTTLEWORTH (1917-1975)
IN BARBON CHURCH VESTRY 1975

IT READS:-

> THE CHIMING APPARATUS
> FOR THE BELLS
> WAS INSTALLED IN MEMORY OF
> CHARLES UGHTRED JOHN
> 4th. BARON SHUTTLEWORTH
> OF GAWTHORPE
> 1917-1975
> BY HIS WIDOW AND CHILDREN

Since 1952 Lord Shuttleworth had been living at Leck Hall
just a few miles from Barbon.

GRAVESTONE OF
LADY ANNE ELIZABETH,
WIFE OF THE
4th. LORD SHUTTLEWORTH
IN BARBON CHURCHYARD 1991

IT READS:-

ANNE ELIZABETH
17th. MARCH 1922
16th. DECEMBER
1991
WIFE of TOM
4th. BARON
SHUTTLEWORTH

Lady Shuttleworth was the
daughter of Colonel Geoffrey
Francis Phillips,
C.B.E., D.S.O.

PAGE 48

GRAVESTONE OF SIR WILLIAM ROUS
SON OF PAMELA née KAY-SHUTTLEWORTH,
GRANDDAUGHTER OF THE 1st. LORD SHUTTLEWORTH,
IN BARBON CHURCHYARD 1999

IT READS:-

LIEUTENANT GENERAL
THE HONOURABLE
SIR WILLIAM ROUS KCB OBE
27TH COLONEL
COLDSTREAM GUARDS
BORN 22ND FEBRUARY 1939
DIED 25TH MAY 1999
JE VIVE EN ESPOIR.

Sir William Rous was first cousin of the
5th. Lord Shuttleworth. He is buried in the Shuttleworth plot.
The French motto is that of the Rouse/Stradbroke family.
The crest above the motto is also from Sir William's family.

THE SHUTTLEWORTHS HELD THE MANOR OF FORCETT, NORTH OF RICHMOND IN YORKSHIRE FOR TWO HUNDRED YEARS, FROM 1582 to 1785

Sir *Richard* (1541-99) and his brother *Thomas* (1546-93) bought the *Manor* and *Estate of Forcett* in 1582-5.

Forcett Hall

Whilst residing at *Forcett Hall*, both *Richard Shuttleworth* (1644-81) and *James Shuttleworth* (1714-73) were *High Sheriffs of Yorkshire*.

The Jacobean *Hall* was remodelled for *Richard* (*Ready Money Dick*) *Shuttleworth* (1683-1749) in c. 1740 by *Daniel Garrett*.

The *Manor* was sold by *Robert Shuttleworth* (1745-1816) in 1785. — *Page 77*

A number of the Shuttleworth family were buried in St. Cuthbert's Church, Forcett, which is situated on the perimeter of the Forcett *Hall* grounds. Three of the Shuttleworth memorials can still be seen on the wall of the South Aisle.

FAMILY TREE OF THOMAS SHUTTLEWORTH (1546-1593)

and ANNE LEVER later UNDERHILL (1587-1669)

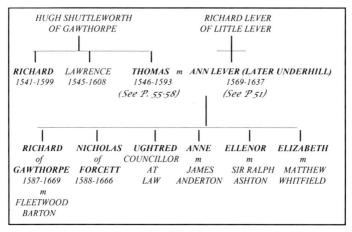

PAGE 50

BRASS MEMORIAL TO ANNE UNDERHILL (1569-1637)
WIDOW OF THOMAS SHUTTLEWORTH (1546-1593)
ON THE SOUTH AISLE OF
ST. CUTHBERT'S CHURCH FORCETT 1637

IT READS:-

WHICH SAYS:-

M   S

LABOUR   *REST*

HERE LIES INTERRED

MRS. ANNE UNDERHILL

DAUGHTER OF RICHARD LEVER

OF LITTLE LEVER IN THE COUNTY OF

LANCASHIRE ESQUIRE, LATE WIFE OF

THOMAS SHUTTLEWORTH ESQUIRE

BY WHOM SHE HAD ISSUE THREE SONS

AND THREE DAUGHTERS VIZ

RICHARD SHUTTLEWORTH OF GAWTHORPE

IN THE SAID COUNTY ESQUIRE

NICHOLAS SHUTTLEWORTH

OF FORCETT ESQUIRE

AND UGHTRED SHUTTLEWORTH ESQUIRE

DECEASED

LATE COUNCELLOR AT LAW

AND ONE OF THE BENCH OF

THE HON: SOCIETY OF LINCOLNS INN.

ANNE MARRIED

JAMES ANDERTON OF CLAYTON

IN THE SAID COUNTY, ESQUIRE

THE LADY ELLENOR MARRIED

SIR RALPH ASHTON OF WHALLEY

IN THE SAID COUNTY, BARONET

AND ELIZABETH MARRIED

MATTHEW WHITFIELD OF WHITFIELD

IN THE COUNTY OF NORTHUMBERLAND,

ESQUIRE.

SHE DEPARTED THIS MORTAL LIFE

IN THE FAITH OF OUR LORD JESUS CHRIST

AND HOPE OF A BLESSED RESURRECTION

TO ETERNAL GLORY

THE 12th. DAY OF MAY AD 1637

BEING OF THE AGE OF 68 YEARS

Death is the way unto life.

Here lyeth interred Ms. Anne Vnderhill

daughter of Richard Leuer of litle Leuer

in the countie of Lanc; Esqr. late wife of Thomas

Shuttleworth Esqr. by whom shee had issue 3 sonnes

& 3 daughters viz: Richard Shuttleworth

of Gawthroppe in ye said county Esqr. Nicholas

Shuttleworth of Forcett Esqr. and Vghtred Shuttle-

worth Esqr. deceased late councellor at lawe

& one of ye Bench of ye Honble. scocietie of Lin-

colns inne. Anne married to James Anderton

of Claiton in ye said countie Esqr.. The Ladie

Ellenor married to Sr. Ralph Ashton of Whalley

in ye said countie, Barronet, & Elizabeth married

to Mathew Whitfeild of Whitfeild in ye countie

of Northumber: Esqr. Shee depted this mortall

life in ye faith of our Lord Jesus Christ & hope of

a blessed resurrection to eternall glory ye 12th. day

of May Ao.Dni. 1637 being of ye age of 68 yeares

Death is the way unto life.

BRASS MEMORIAL INSCRIPTION IN LATIN
TO NICHOLAS SHUTTLEWORTH
SON OF THOMAS (P.55) AND ANNE (P.51) ON THE SOUTH AISLE
OF ST. CUTHBERT'S CHURCH FORCETT 1666

WHEN TRANSLATED IT READS:-

HERE LIES

NICHOLAS SHUTTLEWORTH

OF FORCETT ESQUIRE OF YORK

WHO (ALMOST EIGHTY YEARS OLD)

LEFT THIS LIFE FOR A BETTER ONE

ON THE 20th. DAY OF NOVEMBER 1666.

IN DUTIFUL MEMORY OF HIM, RICHARD SHUTTLEWORTH

DESCENDANT OF THE AFOREMENTIONED NICHOLAS

AND HIS SOLE HEIR,

SET UP THIS MONUMENT

MEMORIAL SARGOPHAGUS
TO JAMES SHUTTLEWORTH (1714-1773)
ON THE SOUTH AISLE OF
ST. CUTHBERT'S CHURCH FORCETT 1773

IT READS:-

IN MEMORY O
JAMES SHUTTLEWORTH ESQ.
WHO BELOVED AND RESPECTED
IN PRIVATE LIFE
SERVED THE PUBLICK IN III PARLIAMENTS
WITH INTEGRITY AND HONOUR.
HE MARRIED MARY DAUGHTER OF
ROB. HOLDEN ESQ. OF DERBYSHIRE
BY WHOM HE LEFT ISSUE
FOUR SONS AND TWO DAUGHTERS.
HE DIED JUNE XXVIII MDCCLXXIII
AGED LVIII.

MEMORABILIA

SMITHILLS HALL, BOLTON, LANCASHIRE
WAS THE HOME OF
SIR RICHARD SHUTTLEWORTH (1541-1599)
AFTER HIS MARRIAGE TO
MARGERY BARTON (nee LEGH) IN 1582

Smithills Hall

Sir Richard Shuttleworth (c1541-1599) married Margery Barton during the lifetime of his father, Hugh Shuttleworth of Gawthorpe. Richard, who was Hugh's eldest son and heir, resided at Smithills by virtue of his wife Margery. She was the widow of the previous Lord of the Manor, Robert Barton who had died in 1580. Margery (or Margaret) was the daughter of Sir Piers Legh of Lyme Hall. As Chief Justice of Chester Richard would frequently be found on his circuit in Cheshire, leaving as his steward at Smithills his youngest brother Thomas who kept the Household Accounts in great detail. After Margery's death in 1592 Smithills was leased to Sir Richard until his death in 1599 when it reverted to the Barton family. Thomas died in 1593 and was buried in Bolton Parish Church. (See P. 55). Sir Richard came into possession of the Gawthorpe Estate and Shuttleworth lands on the death of his father, Hugh, in 1596 and these, in turn, were inherited by his nephew, Thomas' son, Richard -later Colonel - (See P.61) in 1599 when Sir Richard died childless.

PAGE 54

THE HIDDEN TOMBSTONE
IN BOLTON PARISH CHURCH OF
THOMAS SHUTTLEWORTH (1546-1593)

Thomas Shuttleworth, (1546-1593) acted as Steward for his brother **Sir Richard Shuttleworth** and kept the house and farm accounts for him.

Thomas lived at Smithills Hall, Bolton and after his demise in 1593 was recorded in the Parish Register of St. Peter's Parish Church as being buried in the Chancel of the church there. Unfortunately this tomb is now hidden some three feet below the present floor and the inscriptions do not appear to have been recorded.

As Sir Richard did not have an heir it was Thomas' son, **Richard** (later to become **Colonel Richard**) who inherited the Shuttleworth Estates.

The Parish Register states:-
'Thomas Shuttleworth, Gentyl-man buried in the chancell 14 Dec. 1593'.

The Bolton local historian Ron Smith states that this was a 'moonlight funeral' with a torchlight procession from Smithills Hall to the Parish Church.

St. Peter's
Bolton-le-Moors

Thomas' wife, Anne, remarried and in 1637 she was buried at St. Cuthbert's Church, Forcett, north of Richmond, Yorkshire. Her Monumental Inscription as 'Anne Underhill' appears on page 51.

Thomas' will is recorded in 'Bolton Wills' and is reproduced on the following pages:-

WILL OF THOMAS SHUTTLEWORTH , GENTLEMAN,
OF SMITHILLS, BOLTON , LANCASHIRE. 1593

IN THE NAME Of God Amen the fyve & twentithe day of September in the Yeare of our Lord God one thousand fyve hundreth Nyntie three and in the fyve and Thirtith Yeare of the reigne of our Soveraigne Ladie Elizabeth, by the grace of God quene of England Fraunce and Ireland, defender of the Faith &c. I **Thomas Shuttleworthe** of Smithells in the countie of l ancaster g entleman doe ordeyne and m ake this m y laste Will and Testament in manner and forme Followinge. That ys to saye, Firste and principallie I geve and bequeath my Soule unto allmightie God throughe Whose goodnes and mercie I trust to be one of them shalbe Saved, and my bodie I bequeath to Christian Buriall.

Item I will that all my goods, Debtes, duties sommes of money, and Cattells whatsoever (the leases and termes of Yeares i n Ightenhill p arke hereafter expressed, onelie excepted) shall after my decease bee devided into three equal partes.

Whereof the Firste parte I geve and bequeath unto **Ann my Wyffe** in the Name of her Reasonable part of my goodes, Accordinge to the Custome of the Countie.

The seconde parte I geave and bequeath unto **Nycholas Shuttleworth** and **Ughtrede Shuttleworth** my sonnes; **Ann Shuttleworth, Elenor Shuttleworthe** and **Elizabethe Shuttleworthe** my daughters, equallie to be devided amongeste them, for and in the name of theire Reasonable Chyldes partes and porcions of my goodes Accordinge to the Custome aforesaide.

And the thirde and last parte I geave and Bequeath in manner and forme Folowinge. That ys to saye. I geave and Bequeath unto **Hughe Shuttleworth** my father, my beste Cloke and velvett gyrdie. Item to **Sir Richard Shuttleworth** knighte, my brother, Foure Poundes in goulde to make him a Rynge of golde. Item to **Lawrence Shuttleworth** my brother, parson of Whichford, my gould rynge or Signett of golde. Item to my Sister **Jane Shuttleworth**, fourtie shillings. Item I geave unto my Cosin **Henrie Shuttleworth** of grays inne fourtie shillings Yearlie, to be paide unto him duringe the space of thre Yeares nexte after my decease, if he continewe leaveinge in grays Inn aforesaide, otherwise this legacie to be voyd.

Item to **Richard Leaver**, my father in lawe, **Thomas Leaver** his sonne, **Thomassyn** Wyffe of the said **Thomas and Rauffe Leaver**, sonne of the saide Richard Leaver, everie of theym tenne shillings in golde. Item to my Cosins **Thomas Grymshawe**, and **Cuthbert Hesketh**, everie of theyme tenn shillings. Item to **John Woodroffe, William Kenion** and **Robert Aspden**, everie of them ten shillings. Item to everie Servant that weareth my said brother **Sir Richard**, his clothe, fyve shillings and unto everye other his hyred worke servante, aswell men as women, twoe shillings. Item unto **James Yate**, one quarters wage and a paire of hoose and dublett.

PAGE 56

Item I will that my executors shall make pennie dowle unto the poore beinge at my Funerall. Item I geave and bequeath unto the poore people inhabitinge and dwellinge in Padiham and Burneley. To be distributed and devided at the descrecion of my executors. Viz., in Padiham fourtie shillings and in Burnley Twentie shillings and the Resydue of my saide parte and porcion (yf any Remayne) I geave and bequeathe unto my saide Children **Nycholas, Ughtrede, Anne, Elenor and Elizabeth**, equallye to be devyded amongest them.

And forsmuche as I doubte whether the said third parte will Suffice for the payment of my said Legasies and for that, the said Seconde parte will not Suffice for the preferringe of my Children (A reasonable Jointure and dowre beinge allreadie made and provided by me, to and for, my said Wyffe) Therefore my mynde will and intent ys that my executors shall in convenient tyme after my decease, bargayne an sell, graunte or assigne, all such interests and terms of Yeares whatsoever Which I have of and in all those three Messuages and tenements With thappurtenances, lyinge and beinge in Ightenhill parke in the said countie of Lancaster nowe or laite in the severall tenures or occupations of **Roberte Barcrofte** of Ightenhill parke aforesaide, and **Lawrence Spencer** deceased, or of their or either of theire assignee or assignes and of and in all landes & groundes whatsoever to the said Messuage & tenements or any of them belonginge, unto suche person or persons and in suche Manner and Forme as my said executors shall thinke moste expedient, and the money to be receaved of suche Bargayne, Sale graunte or assignment, or of the issues and profytts arrysinge or comminge of or in the said premisses, or any parte therof, before the same Bargayne, Sale graunte or assignement mayde, I will that my executors shall imploye and bestowe for and towards the payment and dischardge of suche of my saide Legasies as shall remayne undischardged with the said thirde parte of my goodes as aforesaide. And the residue of the same Money I geave and be-queath unto the said **Nycholas, Ughtrede, Ann, Elenor** and **Elizabeth**, my son-nes and doughters, equallie to be devided and bestowed amongeste them.

AND wheras the saide **Ann my Wyffe** is Intytled have for her dower the third parte of all my landes and tenements in the countie of Westmorland, nowe yt ys my mynd, will and intente, And I doe gyve, devise and bequeath by theis presentes aswell the revercion of the said thirde parte of my said landes and tenements in Westmorland aforesaid, to be assigned or allotted unto her in dower as aforesaide imedyatile after her decease, as all so the other twoe partes of all my landes and tenements in Westmorland aforesaid, Immediatlie after my decease, unto my executors and theire assignes so longe and untill suche tyme as my executors or the Survyver of them or the executors or assignes of the Survyver of them, shall or maye have receyved of the issues and profitts of the same premisses, suche somme and sommes of money as shall Suffice aswell for the Mayntenaunce and educacion of **Richard Shuttleworth**, my sonne and heire apparent, as to my said executors or to the Survyver of them, or to the executors or assignes of the Survyver of them, shalbe thought expedient, as allso to make uppe the Chyldes partes, porcions and payments before geven, mencioned, appointed or Intended to be paid, unto the saide **Nycholas, Ughtred, Ann, Elenor** and **Elizabeth**, the Juste and full somme of one hundreth poundes a peece for and towardes theire preferment and advancemente.

PROVIDED a llwayes a nd my mynde a nd will ys, t hat yf a ny o f my said Children, viz., **Nycholas, Ughtred, Ann, Elenor** and **Elizabeth** fortune to dye before they shall bee prefered in Marriage or otherwise; or before the receipte of the s aid l egacies o r s ommes o f money b efore mencioned, T hat t hen t he p arte o f porcion, partes or porcions, of suche of them the said **Nycholas, Ughtred, Ann, Elenor** and **Elizabeth**, as so shall dye as aforesaid, shall wholie remayne and bee unto suche of them as shall survive as aforesaid.

Provided further, and my mynd and Will ys that yf any of my Children, that ys to saye, **Nycholas, Ughtred, Ann, Elenor & E lizabeth** will not b e o rdered, ruled or governed by my said brother, **Sir Richard Shuttleworth** or by his appointment, That then his or theire parte and porcion, partes and porcions, before in these presentes mencioned, shallbe improved and bestowed by my saide executors, or the Survyver of them, to such of theme the said **Nycholas, Ughtred, Ann, Elenor** and **Elizabeth**, as my said brother Sir Richard shall lymitt or appointe

And I doe ordeyne, Constitute and make the said **Sir Richard Shuttleworth** knighte, **John Woodroffe, Thomas Grymshawe** and **Nycholas Grymshawe**, Servants of the said **Sir Richard**, executors of this my laste will and testament as my speciall truste ys in them; humblie prayinge the said **Sir Richard** to stand goode unckle to my said Children and for Gods cause to respecte theire educacion. IN WITTNES w hereof hereunto, I the said **Thomas Shuttleworth** have sett m y hand and Seale, Geven the daye and yeare firste above written.

thomas Shuttleworth

ENDORSED. Sealed signed and published the daye and yeare Within specifyed, in the presence of:

William Kenion	**Chistopher Smithe**
Edward Sherburn	**James yeate**
Roberte Aspden	

From 'Bolton Wills and Inventories' by the Bolton and District Family History Society.

EXAMPLE OF THE LAND TRANSACTIONS
OF THOMAS SHUTTLEWORTH
FROM THE
COURT ROLLS OF CLITHEROE 1570

HALMOT COURT OF THE MANOR OF IGHTENHILL 1570

Ingram Willysell of Scolebancke surrendered by Robert Roe, a tenant of the Queen, one close or parcel of land, late parcel of one close called le Great Feilde, previously divided from the same close, containing 6 acres in Padiham, now or lately in the tenure of Thomas Shutleworth, son of Hugh Shotleworthe of Galthropp, to the said Thomas Shutleworth and his assigns for six years from the feast of the Annunciation of the Blessed Virgin Mary (25th. March) in the twelfth year of the reign of our lady Elizabeth now Queen (1570). Admittance sought and granted. Fine 2s. by the pledge of Hugh Shutleworth, gent.

Note:-
The Scholebank Estate was later purchased by the Shuttleworths from Ingram Wyllysell (Willysell) in 1586 for a sum in hand plus an annuity.

The above example is taken from 'The Court Rolls of Clitheroe. 1568-1571' transcribed by John Simpson.

COLONEL RICHARD SHUTTLEWORTH
(SON OF THOMAS, PAGES 55-58)
1587-1669

1621 and 1637.   **Richard Shuttleworth** was High Sheriff of Lancashire.

1633   He was involved in the examinations of Lancashire Witches. (See Page 62).

1641.   As Member of Parliament for Preston he was enjoined by the House of Commons to see the Ordinance of the Militia put in force in Lancashire. (An example of a muster for training can be seen on Page. 63)

1641.   Richard was made a Colonel in the Parliamentary Army in command of the hundred of Blackburn, being wounded in Colne in 1644.

1646.   He was one of the laymen of the 3rd. Lancashire Presbyterian Classis.

1650   As an Ecclesiastical Commissioner, a Colonel for the Parliament and an active Magistrate of the County he was one of the sequestrators of the estates of 'notorious delinquents' in Lancashire and an auditor of the treasurer's accounts. Thus, as an M.P., a puritan in power, an ecclesiastical commissioner, a military commander and a sequestrator for the Roundheads, he incurred the dislike of the Royalists who gave him the nickname of 'Old Smoot'. This slight would be enhanced, no doubt, by the knowledge that he also had a 'second wife' (p 61) Judith Thorpe, by whom he had his nine younger children (1617 to 1628), as he stated at Dugdale's Visitation in 1664. (His first wife Fleetwood was still alive, dying in 1664).

During the Commonwealth, as one of the J.P's for the county of Lancashire and a hymeneal priest (one solemnising marriages), he officiated in that capacity to bind couples together in matrimony. This, of course did not endear him to the local clergy and parishioners. He died in 1669 and is buried in Padiham.

On pages 64 to 72 are examples of these marriages from local Parish Registers.

FAMILY TREE OF
COLONEL RICHARD SHUTTLEWORTH (1587-1669)

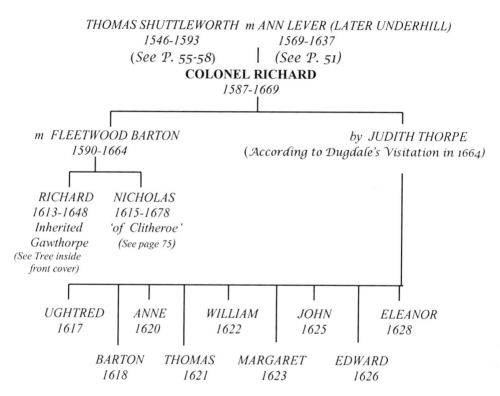

THOMAS SHUTTLEWORTH m ANN LEVER (LATER UNDERHILL)
1546-1593   1569-1637
(See P. 55-58) | (See P. 51)
COLONEL RICHARD
1587-1669

m FLEETWOOD BARTON   by JUDITH THORPE
1590-1664   (According to Dugdale's Visitation in 1664)

RICHARD   NICHOLAS
1613-1648   1615-1678
Inherited   'of Clitheroe'
Gawthorpe   (See page 75)
(See Tree inside
front cover)

UGHTRED   ANNE   WILLIAM   JOHN   ELEANOR
1617   1620   1622   1625   1628

BARTON   THOMAS   MARGARET   EDWARD
1618   1621   1623   1626

Colonel Richard appears to have had a 'second wife' according
to his declaration to Dugdale on the Herald's Visitation in 1664,
the year of his wife Fleetwood's death.
To Fleetwood was attributed the heir and 'the spare'
whilst to Judith Thorpe, daughter of Jeremiah Thorpe
of Bradford, Yorkshire was attributed the other nine children.
Nevertheless, in his will, Richard even classed
Nicholas (the 'spare') as a 'Natural Son'.

EXCERPT FROM EXAMINATION OF A
SUSPECTED 'PENDLE WITCH' BY
RICHARD SHUTTLEWORTH J.P. (later COLONEL) IN 1633

The Examination of Edmund Robinfon *Son of* Edmund Robinfon *of* Pendle-Foreft *eleven years of age, taken at* Padham *before* Richard Shutleworth *and* John Starkey *Efquires, two of his Majefties Juftices of the Peace within the County of* Lancafter, *the* 10th *day of* February, 1633.

"WHO upon Oath informeth, being examined concerning
"the great meeting of the Witches of *Pendle*, faith that
"upon *All-Saints-day* laft paft, he this Informer being
"with one *Henry Parker* a near door-neighbour to him in *Wheatley-*
"*lane*, defired the faid *Parker* to give him leave to gather fome
"Bulloes which he did ; In gathering whereof he faw two Gray-
"hounds, *viz.* a black and a brown ; o1e came running over the
"next field towards him, he verily thinking the one of them to be
"Mr. *Nutters*, and the other to be Mr. *Robinfons*, the faid Gen-
"tlemen then having fuch like. And faith, the faid Grayhounds
"came to him, and fawned on him, they having about their necks
"either of them a Collar, unto each of which was tied a ftring : which
"Collars (as this Informer affirmeth) did fhine like Gold. And he
"thinking that fome either of Mr. *Nutters* or Mr. *Robinfons* Fa-
"mily fhould have followed them, yet feeing no body to follow
"them, he took the fame Gray-hounds thinking to courfe with
"them. And prefently a Hare did rife very near before him. At
"the fight whereof he cried, Loo, Loo, Loo : but the Doggs
"would not run. Whereupon he being very angry took them,
"and with the ftrings that were about their Collars, tied them to
"a little bufh at the next hedge, and with a fwitch that he had in
"his hand he beat them. And in ftead of the black Grayhound
"one *Dickenfons* Wife ftood up, a Neighbour whom this Informer
"knoweth. And inftead of the brown one a little Boy, whom this
"Informer knoweth not. At which fight this Informer being a-
"fraid, endeavoured to run away : but being ftayed by the Wo-
"man (*viz.*) by *Dickenfons* Wife, fhe put her hand into her pocket,
"and pulled forth a piece of Silver much like to a fair fhilling, and
"offered to give him it to hold his tongue and not to tell : which
"he refufed, faying, Nay thou art a Witch. Whereupon fhe put
"her hand into her pocket again, and pulled out a thing like un-
"to a Bridle that gingled, which fhe put on the little Boyes head :
"which faid Boy ftood up in the likenefs of a white Horfe, and in
• the brown Grayhounds ftead. Then immediately *Dickenfons*
Y y 2 'Wife

Page from the original edition of John Webster's book 'The Displaying of Supposed Witchcraft'

The Shuttleworths were also involved in the earlier 'Pendle Witch' Saga, in fact 'Chattox' and her family lived on Shuttleworth land in West Close.

LETTER TO
COLONEL RICHARD SHUTTLEWORTH
REGARDING THE MUSTER OF BURNLEY PARISH
FOR TRAINING. 31st. OCTOBER 1642

FROM JOHN BRADDYLL TO **RICHARD SHUTTLEWORTH**.

To the **Wor**ll **Richard Shuttleworth Esqr.** At Gauthropp, thes ʳsent..

Sʳ.— Mʳ Halstead of Roley & my selfe hath had some Conference to day concerning the calling together of Burnley parish men for to bee exercised & trained tomorrow, as was ordered by yʳ selfe and Mr. Starkie the last day; he denyeth to take that office vpon him, vnless he haue some other helpe for the disciplining of the people; therefore I thought it very meete to aquainte yᵘ that hee would have some other day appointed by yʳ selfe after tomorrow, for meeting & calling the parish together, for hee desires mee to instruct him & bee wᵗʰ him that day, wᶜʰ I am very willing in to my power. I haue sent a pʳcept to Sir reeve of Pendle that all bee ready att New Church after morning prayer, to be in a little readynesse, as the day will suffer after; soe, desiring yʳ answer by this bearer, beinge unwilling to doe anythinge wᵗʰout yʳ consent, remembring my best respecte, euʳ I rest

Yᵒʳ assured to his power

John Braddill

Worsthorne, vltimʳ Octobris 1642

LETTER WRITTEN EARLY IN THE CIVIL WAR WHEN
COLONEL RICHARD SHUTTLEWORTH COMMANDED
THE HUNDRED OF BLACKBURN TOGETHER WITH
COLONEL STARKIE OF HUNTROYDE.

This is one of a number of letters referring to Colonel Richard
which are to be found in the Chetham Society publications on the
Lancashire Lieutenancy under the Tudors and Stuarts.

EXAMPLE FROM THE REGISTER
OF St. LEONARD'S CHURCH, PADIHAM
OF THE MARRIAGES SOLEMNIZED
AT GAWTHORPE HALL BY
COLONEL RICHARD SHUTTLEWORTH 1656

St. Leonard's
Padiham

IT READS:-

The marriage betweene James Calverley and Mary
Barber was solemnised att Gawthropp by **Coll Rich**:
Shutleworth in the pe/sence of John Speake the
elder Mathew Calverley John Calverley and
divers others
The Seaventh day of Aprill 1656./
RIC: SHUTTLEWORTHE

EXAMPLE FROM THE REGISTERS

OF ST. BARTHOLOMEW'S CHURCH, COLNE

AND ST. PETER'S CHURCH, BURNLEY

OF A MARRIAGE OF PARISHIONERS

OF BURNLEY AND COLNE

SOLEMNIZED BOTH AT GAWTHORPE HALL

AND ST. PETER'S BURNLEY BY

COLONEL RICHARD SHUTTLEWORTH 1657

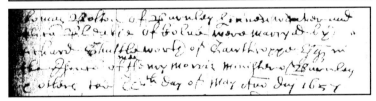

THE COLNE REGISTER READS: -

Thomas Boulton of Bornley, Inkeper, sone of William Boulton deceased and Alice Blakey of Colne spinster, daughter of Joseph Blakey deceased, was married at Gautharop by **Mr. Shutleworth** May ye 11, 1657

THE BURNLEY REGISTER READS :-

Thomas Bolton, Burnley, linnen weaver and Alice Bleakie, Colne, were married by **Richard Shuttleworth** of Gawthroppe Esqr. in the presence of Mr. Henry Morris, minister of Burnley, and others on the 25th. of May Anno Dmi. 1657

EXAMPLES FROM THE REGISTER
OF St. PETER'S CHURCH, BURNLEY
OF THE MARRIAGES SOLEMNIZED BY
COLONEL RICHARD SHUTTLEWORTH 1653/6

St.
Peter's
Burnley

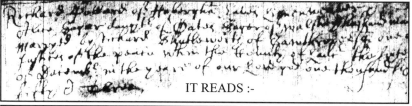

IT READS :-

Richard Pollard of Habergham Eaves linnen weaver and Alice Sagar daughter of
Oates Sager of Walshey husbandman Marryed by **Richard Shuttleworth** of
Gawthroppe Esq. one of the justices of the peace w'hin the county of Lancs.
The sixteenth of December in the year of our Lord God
one thousand six hundred fifty and three

IT READS :-

Francis Horsfall of Cliviger tanner and Mary Weaver, of Burnley, wid: both of the parish of
Burnley married fourteenth of February 1655(6) by **Richard Shuttleworth** of Gawthroppe,
Esqre., one of the justices of the peace for Lancs. County.
Publication first made in the Church of Burnley according to an Act of Parliament.

PAGE 66

EXAMPLES FROM THE REGISTER
OF St. BARTHOLOMEW'S CHURCH, COLNE
OF THE MARRIAGES SOLEMNIZED AT GAWTHORPE
AND AT 'BARNSET' (BARNSIDE?) BY
COLONEL RICHARD SHUTTLEWORTH 1656/7

St.
Bartholomew's
Colne

MARRIED AT GAWTHORPE :-

IT READS :-

Nicholas Michell of Colne, marker, sone of Nicholas Michell deceased and Margret Blakey of Colne spinster, daughter of Joseph Blakey, deceased, was married at Gawtharop by **Mr. Shuttleworth** May ye 11th, 1657

MARRIED AT 'BARNSET' (BARNSIDE?) :-

IT READS :-

Rodger Emott of Barnset, widower, and Ellin Emott of Shawhead widow, was married at Barnset ye 18 day of Aug 1656 by **Mr.Shuttleworth**

PAGE 67

EXAMPLES FROM THE REGISTER
OF St. ANNE'S CHURCH, WOODPLUMPTON
REGARDING THE MARRIAGES SOLEMNIZED THERE
BY COLONEL RICHARD SHUTTLEWORTH 1653/6

St. Anne's, Woodplumpton

N.B.   Colonel Richard himself was married at St. Anne's Woodplumpton in 1612 to Fleetwood Barton, the heiress of Barton Hall, and had thus inherited the Barton Estates.

2nd. MARCH 1653
A Marriage solempnized betweene Thomas Watson son of Nicholas Watson of Plupton, husbandman and Magrett Noblett of Bartell, Spinster
Before **Richard Shuttleworth** Esquire

---

2 APRILL 1656
A marriage solempnized betweene John Brambwell of Woodpluptoon, Husbanman and Marie Aunbie of Woodpluptoon, spinster
Before **Ric: Shuttleworthe** Esquire

---

24 APRILL 1656
A Marriage solempnized betweene William Jolie of Catforth wthin the parish of Woodplupton, Husbanman and Ann All Mon of Catforth
wthin the parish of Woodplumpton, Spinster
Before **Ric: Shuttleworthe** and Edward Robinson

PAGE 68

EXAMPLES FROM THE REGISTER
OF St. JOHN THE BAPTIST CHURCH, BROUGHTON
OF THE MARRIAGES SOLEMNIZED THERE
BY COLONEL RICHARD SHUTTLEWORTH 1654/1657

Boars Head, crest of the Barton Family, with Shuttle, crest of the Shuttleworth family in its mouth, to be seen on a well-weathered stone on the outside wall over the choir vestry of Broughton Church.
Colonel Richard Shuttleworth had married Fleetwood Barton the heiress of Thomas Barton (his initials are shown on the stone, T.B.), in 1612.

St. John the Baptist, Broughton

4TH MAY 1654
John Clarkson of Eaves in Woodplumpton parish and Ellen Whaley of the pishe of Broughton a spinster wth the consent of her father as it was certiffied by the due publication of their purpose of marriage accordinge to the tenor of the late Acte of Parliament were the second day of May 1654 declared to be man and wife before
Richard Shuttleworthe Esquire
Edm: Blacowe Register

25th. OCTOBER 1657
A publication of an intention and purpose of marriage was made 3 severall Lords dayes w[th]in the pishe of Broughton betwene Richard Singleton of Barton husbandman and Elen Shakshaft of Fullwood spinster and a certiffcat made and returned thereof unto **Richard Shuttleworth Esq. Justice of the Peace** the 25 day of October 1657 where upon the same day the marriage before him was solempnized between Richard and Elen in the p[r]sents of John Singleton, William Singleton and div[rs] other witnesses and regestered by me Tho; Blacow

EXAMPLES FROM THE REGISTER
OF St. ANNE'S CHURCH, WOODPLUMPTON AND
OF St. JOHN THE BAPTIST CHURCH, BROUGHTON
REGARDING THE MARRIAGES SOLEMNIZED
AT BARTON LODGE BY
COLONEL RICHARD SHUTTLEWORTH 1656/7

Barton Lodge

RECORDED AT ST. ANNE'S CHUCH, WOODPLUMPTON:-

> ## 10 JULY 1656
> The marriage betweene Christopher Willasie of Catforth wthin the pishe of Woodplumpton, Husbanman and Magrett Miller of Clifton, wthin the pishe of Kirkham, widowe was solempnized at Barton in the presence of Cuthbert Cardewell and William Daniell of Barton Before **Ric: Shuttleworthe**

> ## 26 AUGUST 1656
> The marriage betweene Richard Charnely of Catforth wthin the pish of Woodplumpton, Husbanman and Katharin Hughell of the same, Spinster was Solempnized att Barton in the presence of John Charnely and John Smyth both of Woodplumpton. Before **Ric: Shuttleworthe**

RECORDED AT ST. JOHN THE BAPTIST CHURCH, BROUGHTON:-

> ### 25th. OCTOBER 1657
> A certiffcat of an intention and purpose of marriage in the pochiall church of Brought: betwene Richard Barton and Alieice Hatternate of Durton w[th]in the pishe of Gasstange delivered by me the 30[th] day of November 1657 and weare in the p[r]sents of Richard Cardwell and William Greason the witnesses duely married att Barton before **Richard Shuttleworth Esq. Justice of the Peace** the same day according to the late act of Parliament then registered by me   Thomas Blacowe

EXAMPLES FROM THE REGISTER
OF ALL HALLOWS, MITTON
OF THE MARRIAGES SOLEMNISED BY
COLONEL RICHARD SHUTTLEWORTH 1654

All Hallows, Mitton

17th. APRIL 1654
Samuell Felgate & Elizabeth Walker.
Banns, 25 March, 1 & 8 April.
Married by **Rich: Shuttleworth.**

24th. MAY 1654
James Dewhirst & Mary Winckley.
Banns, 6, 13, & 20 May.
Married by **Rich: Shuttleworth.**

EXAMPLES FROM THE REGISTER
OF St. LEONARD'S CHURCH, DOWNHAM
OF THE MARRIAGES SOLEMNIZED
AT GAWTHORPE HALL BY
COLONEL RICHARD SHUTTLEWORTH 1656/7

St. Leonard's
Downham

13th.MARCH 1656
Alexander Illingworth & Judeth Riley, b.t.c., at Gawthropp by
Coll.Richard Shutleworth.
Wit : Leonard Clarkson, William Crookey.

7th. APRIL 1656
John Speake & Margaret Prockter, b.t.c., at Gawthropp by
Coll.Richard Shutleworth.
Wit. :John Speake the Elder, Matthew Calverley, John Calverley.

7th. APRIL 1656
Thomas Speake & Grace Shackleton, b.t.c. at Gawthropp by
Coll.Richard Shutleworth.
Wit. John Speake the Elder,Matthew Calverley, John Calverley.

9th. JUNE 1657
William Speake & Elezabeath, wid. Henery Bailey, b.t.c. at Gawthropp by
Coll.Richard Shutleworth.
Wit. John Speake, James Whip.

MARRIED AT 'BROCKEFOUT':-

29th. DECEMBER 1657
James Whipp & Mary Boulcocke at Brockefout by
Coll.Richard Shutleworth.
Wit. Robard Boulcocke, Richard Boulcocke

PAGE 72

EXAMPLES FROM THE PARISH REGISTERS OF THE
APPROVAL GIVEN BY COLONEL RICHARD
SHUTTLEWORTH AFTER THE CIVIL WAR FOR THE
APPOINTMENT OF THE PARISH REGISTRAR
AFTER THE REGISTERS WERE RESUMED
BY THE ACT OF 24th. AUGUST 1653

FROM WOODPLUMPTON PARISH REGISTER:-

---

16 FEBRUARY 1653/4

John Turner of Woodplumpton ln the sd Countie Yeoman being chosen by the
Inhabitants and howshoulders of the pochicall Chappelrie of Woodplumpton afforsd
to bee their Register came before me the 16th of Februarie 1653 and was by mee
approued on to bee the Register for the sd pochiall Chapelrie and to haue the keeping
of this booke And was by mee sworne accordinge to the Act of Parliamt of the 24th
of August last past in that behalfe made
Ric: Shuttleworthe

FROM BROUGHTON PARISH REGISTER:-

---

19 NOVEMBER 1657.

Theis are to testifie all whome it maye concerne
That Thomas Blackowe of Barton yeo: being vpon the death of Edmund Blacowe,
his late father deceased dulie elected by the inhabitants of the pishe or Chappelrie
of Broughton to be their pish register, came before mee this day at **Gawthrop**,
and was by mee admitted, allowed and sworne to bee the pishe Register of the
sd pishe or Chappelrie and has the Register bookes thereof deliuered vnto him
according to the Act of the xxiiijth of August 1653.
Wittnes my hand the xixth daie of Nouember 1657
Ric: Shuttleworthe

TOMBSTONE IN THE CHANCEL OF
ST. JAMES CHURCH, ALTHAM
(NEAR PADIHAM) 1744

St. James,
Altham

As the chancel floor has been re-laid this tombstone has been covered and cannot be seen.

HERE LIES THE BODY OF
RALPH SHUTTLEWORTH, GENT.
AND
SUSANNAH HIS WIFE.
SHE WAS THE ONLY DAUGHTER OF
RICHARD GRIMSHAW OF CLAYTON, ESQ.

HE DIED JANUARY 30th. 1733
AND SHE DIED JUNE 13th. 1727.

ALSO THE BODY OF RALPH SHUTTLEWORTH, GENT.
THEIR SON WHO DIED AT ROCHDALE DECEMBER 18th. 1744;
ALSO THE BODY OF NICOLAS SHUTTLEWORTH,
WHO WAS THE SECOND SON OF RALPH,
AND GRANDSON OF
RICHARD GRIMSHAW, OF CLAYTON.
HE DIED MAY 24th. 1704

Ralph, who married Susannah, was the son of Nicholas, the second son of Colonel Richard Shuttleworth of Gawthorpe (see p 75).

THE FAMILY TREE OF
NICHOLAS SHUTTLEWORTH OF
CLITHEROE (P. 74).
BORN 1615

COLONEL RICHARD SHUTTLEWORTH OF GAWTHORPE
1587-1669

COL. RICHARD JNR. (1613-48)	COL. NICHOLAS (1615-1678)
Married JANE KIRKE	'of CLITHEROE'
(Inherited Gawthorpe Hall)	Married MARGARET STANDISH
-See Tree inside cover-	daughter of THOMAS STANDISH of Duxbury

RALPH (1664-1733)
Married SUSANNAH GRIMSHAW (1658-1727)
daughter of RICHARD GRIMSHAW of Clayton

RALPH	NICHOLAS	ANN	EDWARD
(1685-1744)	(1688-1704)	born 1695	born 1698

THE BARTON ESTATE, NORTH OF PRESTON IN LANCASHIRE WAS HELD BY THE SHUTTLEWORTHS FOR OVER TWO HUNDRED YEARS FROM 1612 TO 1833

Barton Lodge / Hall

Barton Lodge was brought into the Shuttleworth family by the heiress Fleetwood Barton on her marriage to Richard Shuttleworth (later a Colonel in the Parliamentary Army) in 1612. It was used as a residence by the family when they were M.P.'s for Lancashire together with a town house in Winckley Square, Preston. (Gawthorpe at this time was not used by the Shuttleworths partly due to the pollution of the river Calder which ran by the Hall.) The Shuttleworth's permanent residence at this time was Forcett Hall near Richmond, in Yorkshire. (See P. 50) James, the eldest son of Robert Shuttleworth (1745-1816) -See pages 77 to 82- inherited Barton Lodge and sold it in 1833. He retired to Lyme Regis, Dorset, and died at Bradford House near Barnstaple, Devon on 22nd. November 1846.

THE INTRIGUING ROBERT SHUTTLEWORTH
GRANDFATHER OF JANET,
(THE SHUTTLEWORTH HEIRESS)
1745-1816

Robert Shuttleworth was the son and heir of **James Shuttleworth** (Memorial P 53).
Sir Roger Fulford, the step-grandfather of the 5th. Lord Shuttleworth, stated that Robert was 'the most intriguing (though possibly not the most reputable) of his family.' He entered Christ Church College, Oxford at the age of 17 and inherited the Shuttleworth Estates on the death of his father in 1773. By 1777 he had already sold part of his inheritance and was living in New Burlington Street in London's West End. He was proposed as a Fellow of the Royal Society and elected to the inner circle, the Royal Society Club. In 1778 he was sworn into the Corporation of Trinity House. He appears to have had a fascination for the sea and yachting in particular.

He married Anne Desaguliers on the 15th. of May 1776 at St. James, Westminster. She was the daughter of General Thomas Desaguliers, equerry to King George 111. They bought Wandon House in Buckinghamshire and rented Gilbury House on Southampton Water in order that he could continue his sailing hobby but later moved to the south bank of the Thames, below Woolwich. He had by now a number of mistresses. (His payments to one of these, Mrs. Saxray, is documented). Due to these extravagances he was forced to sell more of his Shuttleworth inheritance.

He sold **Forcett Hall** in 1785 and purchased a large estate on the island of St. John's (Prince Edward Island) in Canada in 1792. It consisted of 23,496 acres and cost £1,500. He arrived in Charlottetown on 30th. May 1793 (P.78) and was appointed to the Council on the 8th. of June, being commissioned Colonel in the militia on the 28th. He built a Mansion House on his land by the Morrell River. He also bought property in Charlottetown in December and had a two-masted schooner named 'The Morell' built for himself. He later built a grist mill on the stream at Bristol at which his tenants were obliged, by their leases, to have their grain ground. He finally returned to England in 1798.

There is no existing portrait of Robert, the only member of the Shuttleworth line from 1600 whose likeness is unknown. He is known to have given one to a Miss Bowyer but it has never been traced.

Today on the site of Morell House is a potato warehouse.

EXCERPT FROM THE 'ROYAL GAZETTE'

OF PRINCE EDWARD ISLAND, CANADA,

3 JUNE 1793, REFERRING TO

ROBERT SHUTTLEWORTH (1745-1816)

IT READS:-

On the 30th. ult. arrived here, the brig Lewis, Captain William Baker, in five weeks passage from England.

We have the pleasure to announce the safe arrival here of **Robert Shuttleworth,** Esquire, gentleman of great opulence and fortune, and lately become a Proprietor in this island.

This gentleman has brought with him his family, and likewise a master carpenter to superintend the building of a large and elegant Mansion House, which we are informed he intends to erect on his land on the Morrell River, the frame of which is in great forwardness. The necessaries requisite to finish, decorate, and furnish this building were brought by **Mr.** Shuttleworth in the Brig Lewis; which he charted for that purpose.

Courtesy of Prince Edward Island Museum, Canada

Morrell Mansion House. 1795

PAGE 78

DEATH OF ROBERT SHUTTLEWORTH'S
WIFE ANNE (nee DESAGULIERS) IN 1801
AND HIS PURCHASE OF
BELMONT CASTLE IN 1804

DIED.

Yefterday, in Devonfhire-place, Mrs. Shuttleworth, wife of Robert Shuttleworth, of Burton Lodge, in the County of Lancafter, Efq.

ANNOUNCEMENT OF THE DEATH OF ANNE IN 'THE TIMES' OF 24 APRIL 1801

After Anne's death Robert sold his property in Prince Edward Island in 1804. The sale documents carried his seal of 'Three Shuttles with a Crest of an Armoured Arm with the Gauntlet grasping a Shuttle'. At that time he was living in London, at Upper Norton St., Mary-le-Bone.

In the same year, 1804, Robert bought Belmont Castle and its parkland in Grays, Essex, for £7,875. Documents dated July 1804 record the sale. After Robert's death the castle passed to his son, Robert. It was sold by the Shuttleworths about 1822.

Courtesy of Grays Thurrock Museum, Essex

Belmont Castle, Grays, Essex.

HIGH MARBLE PLAQUE WITH MANTEL TO ROBERT SHUTTLEWORTH (1745-1816) IN ORSETT ST. GILES CHURCH ESSEX. 1816

Robert died in London at his home in Upper Norton Street in 1816

> On the 29th ult. at his home in Upper Norton
> street, London, Robert Shuttleworth, Esq. pro-
> prietor of Barton Lodge, near this town, aged 71.

ANNOUNCEMENT OF THE DEATH OF ROBERT SHUTTLEWORTH IN
THE 'PRESTON CHRONICLE' OF 10TH. FEBRUARY 1816

It remains a mystery why he was buried in
Orsett St. Giles Church, Essex.

Marble plaque in Orsett Church.   IT READS:-

SACRED TO THE MEMORY OF
ROBERT SHUTTLEWORTH Esqr.
OF GAWTHORPE HALL AND BARTON LODGE
IN THE COUNTY PALATINE OF LANCASTER
HE DEPARTED THIS LIFE
29TH. DAY OF JANUARY 1816
AGED 71 YEARS
AND HIS REMAINS ARE DEPOSITED
IN THE VAULT NEAR THIS PLACE

BURIAL REGISTER OF ORSETT ST. GILES CHURCH

BURIALS in the Parish of *Orsett* in the County of *Essex* in the Year 1816			
Name.	Abode.	When buried.	Age.	By whom the Ceremony was performed.
Robert Shuttleworth Esquire. No. 66.	Norton Street Mary-la-bone London.	February 3	71.	John Clee Vr. O. Sha. Curate or Cunt.

ROBERT SHUTTLEWORTH'S HATCHMENT
ABOVE THE MARBLE PLAQUE IN
ORSETT ST. GILES CHURCH, ESSEX 1816

 =

This hatchment is in need of restoration.

ARMS:- Quarterly, 1st. & 4th, or, three shuttles sable, (SHUTTLEWORTH) 2nd. & 3rd., or, three boars heads erased sable. (BARTON). Crest:- an arm vested azure, cuffed argent, holding a shuttle sable. Motto:- 'Resurgam'. (I shall rise again.)

Drawn and detailed by Christopher Harrold.

Robert left the Barton Estate (P.76) to his eldest son, James. He left Gawthorpe and other properties including Belmont Castle (P.79) to his second son, Robert. The younger Robert was killed in a carriage accident two years later leaving a year old daughter, Janet Shuttleworth, as his heiress.

THE YOUNGER
ROBERT SHUTTLEWORTH

JANET SHUTTLEWORTH
'THE HEIRESS'
WITH HER MOTHER JANET
(Nee MARJORIBANKS)

PAGE 81

THE LAST WILL AND TESTAMENT OF ROBERT SHUTTLEWORTH ESQ.
OF BARTON LODGE IN THE COUNTY PALATINE OF LANCASTER 1816

I give to my daughters one hundred pounds apiece for mourning and my Brother the **Revd. Charles Holden** and to my Sister **Mrs. Hurt** fifty Guineas each for a ring. I give and devise all and every my manors messuages farms Lands hereditaments and real Estate situate in the Counties of Lancaster and Westmoreland unto and to the use of the Right Honorable **John Lord Crewe** and **Abraham Henry Chambers** of Bond Street in the County of Middlesex Esquire and their heirs upon trust that they or the survivor of them or their heirs and assigns of such survivor do and shall convey settle and assure the same to the uses hereinafter mentioned that is to say to the intent that my daughter **Elizabeth Shuttleworth** do and out of the rents and profits thereof take one annual sum of two hundred and fifty pounds during her life if she shall so long continue single and unmarried the same to be paid to her quarterly at the usual feast days the first payment thereof to be made on the first quarterly day after my decease and subject thereto to the use of trustees to be named in such settlement for a term of five hundred years Intrust by sale Mortgage or other disposition thereof to raise the sum of two thousand seven hundred and seventy seven pounds fifteen shillings and seven pence and pay the same to my said daughter in addition to the provision made for her hereby and by my marriage Settlement with a proviso for determining the said term when the trusts thereof shall be satisfied and subject thereto to the use of my Son **Robert Shuttleworth** his heirs and assigns for ever

I do hereby make constitute and appoint my said Son **Robert Shuttleworth** sole Executor of this my Will and I give to my said Son **Robert Shuttleworth** his heirs Executors Administrators and assigns all my real and personal Estate and Effects whatsoever and wheresoever and of what nature or kind soever after payment of all my just Debts Legacies and funeral Expences. I revoke all other Wills by me at any time heretofore made and declare this only to be my last Will and Testament In witness whereof I the said Robert Shuttleworth have hereunto my hand and Seal and have also set my hand and Seal to a duplicate hereof this twenty fourth day of October in the year of our Lord one thousand eight hundred and fifteen —

Robert Shuttleworth Signed Sealed published and declared by the said testator **Robert Shuttleworth** as and for his Last Will and Testament in the presence of us who in his presence and at his request have subscribed our names as Witnesses thereto —
Edw Robson — S. Furley — W. B. Gough all of Castle Street Leicester Square.

Proved at London 6th. Feby. 1816. before the Worshipful **Richard Henry Cresswell** Doctor of Laws and Surrogate by the Oath of **Robert Shuttleworth Esq.** the son and sole Executor to whom admon was granted being first sworn duly to administer.

Will WRW/A 1833, Lancashire Record Office, with the permission of the County Archivist

THE LAST WILL AND TESTAMENT OF ROBERT SHUTTLEWORTH ESQ.
(SON OF ROBERT SHUTTLEWORTH WHO DIED IN 1816 -P.82-)
OF GAWTHORPE HALL IN THE COUNTY OF LANCASTER 1818

Made the twelfth day of February one thousand eight hundred and eighteen
I direct all my just debts legacies funeral and testamentary expences to be first paid and
satisfied and if my personal Estate shall be insufficient for that purpose then I charge my Real
Estate with the deficiency I desire to be buried in the Church Yard nearest to the place of my
death unless I die in London and then not nearer than fifteen miles but on no account to be
taken to Gawthorpe and in the plainest manner possible I give to all of my brothers and
Sisters fifty pounds apiece to be paid to them soon after my decease I give and bequeath unto
Sir John Marjoribanks of Lees in the County of Berwick Baronet his Executors
Administration and assign all my Goods Chattels and Personal Estate and Effects whatsoever
and wheresoever, except my Household furniture plate and Library of Books and also except
my Chariot which Chariot I hereby give to my dear wife Janet upon trust to sell and dispose of
the same and stand possessed of the money arising from the sale thereof upon the trusts herein
after declare concerning the same. I give and devise unto and to the use of the said **Sir John
Marjoribanks** his heirs and assigns all my Lands Tenements Hereditaments and Real Estate
whatsoever and wheresoever and of what natures or kind soever except my Estate at
Bilsborough in the County of Lancaster upon the trusts and for the intents and purposes
hereinafter expressed and declared concerning the same, that is to say, upon trust by and out
of the rents issues and profits thereof to pay to my faithful servant **Samuel Wright** and his
assigns during his natural life one annuity of one hundred pounds clear of any deduction to be
paid to him half yearly at Midsummer and Christmas the first half yearly payment thereof to be
made on the first of those days which shall next after my demise and upon further trust by and
out of such rents dues and profits to pay to my dear Wife or her assigns during her natural life
one annuity or clear yearly sum of one thousand p ounds o ver and above the one thousand
pounds a year Jointure settled upon her in my Marriage Settlement the same to be clear of any
Deduction to my said dear Wife half yearly at Midsummer and Christmas the first half yearly
payment thereof to be made on the first of those days which shall happen next after my
decease and also do and from and out of such rents issues and profits pay one annual sum of
three hundred pounds half yearly on the day aforesaid for the maintenance and education of
our daughter until she shall attain the age of fifteen years and from that time the annual sum of
five hundred pounds until she shall attain the age of twenty one years and upon further trust
that he the said **Sir John Marjoribanks** his heirs and assigns do and by and out of such rents
issues and profits pay and discharge all Annuities and Interest of Money dues and chargeable
upon my said Estates and from time to time as opportunity may offer to pay off and discharge
all Mortgages and Incumbrances charged thereupon and subject and charged as aforesaid upon
trust that he the said **Sir John Marjoribanks** his heirs and assigns do and shall when and as
soon as my daughter shall attain the age of twenty one years by all necessary conveyances

THE WILL OF ROBERT SHUTTLEWORTH 1818 (cont.)

and assurances convey settle and assure all my said Lands Tenements Hereditaments and Real Estate whatsoever and wheresoever, except my said Estates at Bilsborough aforesaid and all savings and accumulations of Rents issues and profits therefrom to the use of my said daughter for her life without impeachment of waste and with the usual power of leasing for twenty one years under the usual restrictions with remainder to the first and other sons of my said daughter successively in tail Male with remainder to the first and other daughters successively in tail Male with remainder to my brother **James Shuttleworth** for his life with remainder to his first and other sons successively in tail Male with remainder once to such persons and for such estates as the Barton Estate stand settled and limited on the decease of my said Brother without issue Male I will and direct that if my dear Wife should like to live at my house at Gawthorpe that she shall be at liberty so to do as long as she pleases without paying any Rent for the same I direct the said **Sir John Marjoribanks** his Executors and Administrators to stand possessed of the money arising from the sale of my Goods Chattels and personal Estate and Effects hereinbefore directed to be sold and also the Rent of my House and premises at Gawthorpe in case my dear Wife shall not chuse to reside there upon trust to apply the same in like manner and for the same purposes as I have hereinbefore directed concerning the rents and profits of my Real Estate I direct all my household furniture plate and Library of Books to be held and enjoyed by the person for the time being in possession of my Real Estate in the nature of heir looms as long as the Rules of Law and Equity will admit I give and devise all my Real Estate at Bilsborough in the county of Lancaster unto the said **Sir John Marjoribanks** and his heirs to the use of my brother **James Shuttleworth Esq.** of Barton Lodge and his heirs for his life with remainder to the said **Sir John Marjoribanks** and his heirs during the life of my said Brother in trust to preserve the contingent remainders with remainder to the first and other sons of my said brother successively in tail Male with such remainders over as the Barton Estates now stand settled and limited in failure of issues Male of my said Brother I hereby appoint and constitute the said **Sir John Marjoribanks** and my said dear Wife Executor and Executrix of this my last Will and Testament In witness whereof I have hereunto set my hand and seal the day and year first above written

Robert Shuttleworth

Signed sealed published and declared by the said **Robert Shuttleworth** the Testator as and for his last Will and Testament in the presence of us who in his presence at his request and in the presence of each other have hereunto subscribed our names as Witnesses thereof—
Edwd. Robson—E. Davies—W. B. Gough— all of Castle Street, Leicester Square.

Proved at London 27th May 1818 before the Worshipful **Samuel Pearse**, Parson Doctor of Law and Surrogate by the Oath of **Sir John Marjoribanks** Baronet one of the Executors to whom Admon was granted having been first sworn duly to administer power reserved to **Janet Shuttleworth** widow the Relict the other Executor.

BURNLEY CORN MILL NOTICE WITH THE
'INFANT HEIRESS' JANET SHUTTLEWORTH (1817-1872)
NAMED AS THE PROPRIETOR 1836

Burnley Mill.

Whereas,

Divers Persons who owe Suit at the Ancient Mill called Burnley Mill, situate in the Township of *Burnley*, in the County Palatine of Lancaster, have lately neglected to do Suit at the said Mill, and have ground Wheat, Beans, Oats, Barley, or other Grain, or made Oats into Groats, or ground Groats into Meal, or made or ground Malt, or have carried their Grist to other Mills, contrary to the Rights, Privileges, and Prerogatives of the said Ancient Mill, and contrary to the Ancient Custom there. Now we the Undersigned, Attornies, as well of *Thomas Woodhead*, the present Miller and Farmer of the said Ancient Mill, as of *Janet Shuttleworth*, an Infant, and of the Trustee and Guardian of the said Infant, the Proprietors of the said Ancient Mill, do hereby give you Notice, that Proceedings at Law will be taken against all Persons whomsoever owing Suit at the said Mill who shall henceforth neglect to perform the same according to the Ancient and Lawful Custom. And that a Copy of the Letters Patent of his late Majesty King *James the First*, under the Great Seal of England, and of the County Palatine of Lancaster, and the Seal of the Duchy of Lancaster, bearing date at Westminster, the Eleventh Day of February, in the 7th Year of his said Majesty's Reign, is deposited with *Mr. James Whittaker*, the Agent of the Proprietors, at Gawthorpe Hall, within Habergham Eaves, in the said County, for the perusal and inspection of all Persons interested in the same. Dated the *Twelfth* Day of *March*, 1836.

To the *Inhabitants of the
Townships of Burnley*
and *Habergham Eaves*.

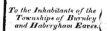 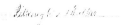

Janet Shuttleworth, the heiress of Robert Shuttleworth who died in 1818 (p. 83) was born in 1817 so she would be in her nineteenth year at the time that this notice was issued.
The problem was that three steam corn mills had opened since 1800 in opposition to the old King's Mill 'contrary to ancient custom.'
Action was taken against a number of people for contravening these rights, including two Greenwood brothers who had originally worked at the old soke mill before opening their own steam driven power mill. In 1842 Janet Shuttleworth married Dr. James Phillips Kay.

PAGE 85

SIR JAMES PHILLIPS KAY-SHUTTLEWORTH
THE CELEBRATED VICTORIAN EDUCATIONALIST 1804-1877

James Phillips Kay was born in Rochdale in **1804** to a manufacturing family and was baptised at Bamford chapel in February 1805. He worked for three years in his uncle's bank, Fenton and Roby's in Rochdale and became Superintendent of the boy's Sunday school at Bamford Chapel. Reading and Writing were the main subjects. His aunt, Ann Fenton (nee Kay) had provided all the books for the school. In 1824 he became a medical student in Edinburgh and graduated in 1827. He practised in Manchester from 1828 to 1835 and was working in Manchester and Salford during the cholera epidemic of 1832.

In **1835** James became an Assistant Poor Law Commissioner and this convinced him of the need for a national system of education and teacher training.

1839 was appointed secretary to the Committee of the Privy Council on Education.

In **1839/40** he founded the first teacher training college in Battersea, London, with E. Carleton Tufnell. Kay established school inspections and expanded the pupil teacher system. Matthew Arnold stated that he was 'the founder of English popular education'.

After **Janet Shuttleworth, the heiress of Gawthorpe,** wrote to James for advice regarding the staffing of the school that she had extended at Habergham (Pages 94/95) they corresponded and finally married in **1842**. He assumed her surname and became **James Phillips Kay-Shuttleworth** at this time.

In **1847** the Kay-Shuttleworths provided the land plus £1,300 and the Dugdales added £3,000 to build Habergham Church. James' health broke down in 1849 and upon his enforced retirement he was created a baronet.

In **1850** he turned his attention to Gawthorpe Hall and commissioned the architect Sir Charles Barry to plan the alterations. It was in this year, too, that the Kay-Shuttleworths invited Charlotte Bronte to visit the Hall for the first time.

Two years after the birth of their fifth child in 1851 Janet left James and never saw the completed renovation of Gawthorpe. She lived mainly on the Continent.

In **1862**, at the time of the Cotton Famine, James was appointed Secretary of the Cotton Districts Relief Fund and Vice Chairman of the Central Executive Committee.. He was appointed High Sheriff of Lancashire in 1864, wrote a number of papers on Education and also two novels. He continued to live at the Hall and at their house at 38, Gloucester Square, London until Janet's death in Germany in 1872 when he moved to Barbon Manor as his son Ughtred inherited Gawthorpe. **James Phillips Kay-Shuttleworth** died in London on 26th. May **1877** and is buried in Brompton Cemetery. (East Position, Compartment 5).

FAMILY TREE OF JAMES PHILLIPS KAY

THE KAY FAMILY
Originally of Bass Lane, Walmersley, Bury, Lancs.

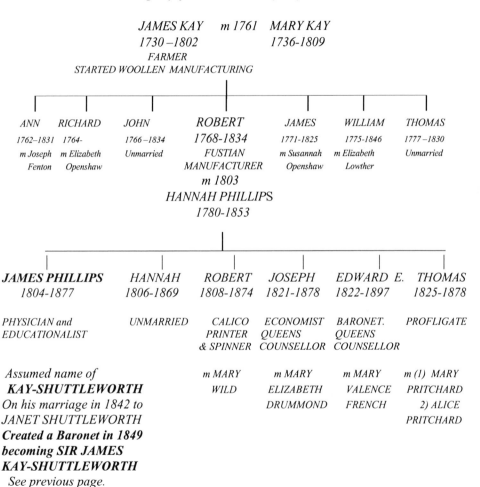

JAMES KAY   m 1761   MARY KAY
1730 –1802   1736-1809
FARMER
STARTED WOOLLEN MANUFACTURING

ANN	RICHARD	JOHN	ROBERT	JAMES	WILLIAM	THOMAS
1762–1831	1764-	1766 –1834	1768-1834	1771-1825	1775-1846	1777 –1830
m Joseph	m Elizabeth	Unmarried	FUSTIAN	m Susannah	m Elizabeth	Unmarried
Fenton	Openshaw		MANUFACTURER	Openshaw	Lowther	
			m 1803			
			HANNAH PHILLIPS			
			1780-1853			

JAMES PHILLIPS	HANNAH	ROBERT	JOSEPH	EDWARD E.	THOMAS
1804-1877	1806-1869	1808-1874	1821-1878	1822-1897	1825-1878
PHYSICIAN and	UNMARRIED	CALICO	ECONOMIST	BARONET.	PROFLIGATE
EDUCATIONALIST		PRINTER	QUEENS	QUEENS	
		& SPINNER	COUNSELLOR	COUNSELLOR	
Assumed name of		m MARY	m MARY	m MARY	m (1) MARY
KAY-SHUTTLEWORTH		WILD	ELIZABETH	VALENCE	PRITCHARD
On his marriage in 1842 to			DRUMMOND	FRENCH	2) ALICE
JANET SHUTTLEWORTH					PRITCHARD
Created a Baronet in 1849					
becoming SIR JAMES					
KAY-SHUTTLEWORTH					
See previous page.					

MEMORIAL TO JAMES KAY (1730-1802)
GRANDFATHER OF
SIR JAMES PHILLIPS KAY-SHUTTLEWORTH
IN PARK CHAPEL, WALMERSLEY, BURY 1802

Park Congregational Chapel,
Walmersley, Ramsbottom, near Bury,
Lancashire closed in 2001 and the
future of the building is uncertain
although internments still take place
there in the adjoining graveyard.

THE TABLET TO THE RIGHT
OF THE PULPIT READS:-

SACRED TO THE MEMORY OF
JAMES KAY OF BASS LANE, WHO DEPARTED
THIS LIFE FEBRUARY THE 16TH, 1802
AGED 71 YEARS.
ALSO OF MARY HIS WIFE WHO DEPARTED
THIS LIFE SEPTEMBER THE 3RD, 1809
AGED 72 YEARS.
ALSO OF THOMAS KAY OF BASS LANE, THEIR SON,
WHO DEPARTED THIS LIFE MARCH THE 13TH, 1830
AGED 53 YEARS.
ALSO OF JOHN KAY OF LARK HILL, THEIR SON,
WHO DEPARTED THIS LIFE MARCH THE 25TH, 1834
AGED 68 YEARS.

James (born 1730), his wife Mary (born 1737), and sons Thomas (born 1777), John (born 1766)

James Kay and his wife were interred beneath the 'Singing Pew' in Park Chapel.
He appears to have been the principal founder of the Chapel.
All their sons, except Robert, father of Sir James Kay-Shuttleworth (see Page 86)
are buried in the chapel (see next page).

The Kay family were living in Bass House, Walmersley, as early as 1549
when a John Kay of that address (aged 72) is noted as a witness in the
Duchy Court of the 8th. of July in that year.

MEMORIAL TO JAMES KAY (1771-1825)
UNCLE OF
SIR JAMES PHILLIPS KAY-SHUTTLEWORTH
IN PARK CHAPEL, WALMERSLEY, BURY 1825

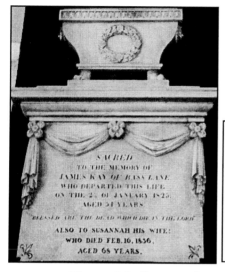

James Kay and his brothers were all First Trustees of Park Chapel where their father, James (see previous page) appeared to have been the principal founder.

THE TABLET TO THE LEFT
OF THE PULPIT READS:-

> Sacred
> To the memory of
> James Kay of Bass Lane
> Who departed this life
> On the 2nd of January, 1825
> Aged 54 years.
> " Blessed are the dead which die in the Lord."
> Also to Susannah his wife,
> Who died Feb. 16th, 1836
> Aged 68 years.

These, with Thomas, John, Richard and five other members of the Kay family were interred in the Kay vaults under the old Vestry, (the present vestibule). Probably the Vaults had not been completed at the time of James the Elder's death in 1802.

James (born 1771), was the uncle of Sir James Kay-Shuttleworth and the son of James and Mary (previous page). He was a woollen manufacturer. Susannah (born 1768), his wife, was the daughter of James Openshaw of Redivales. Their daughter Mary married John Fort M.P. of Read Hall.

The first Trustees of Park Chapel included the Kay brothers James and Thomas, merchants of Bass Lane, together with Richard and his son (also called Richard) merchants in Limefield, Bury, John, a merchant in Lark Hill, and William a merchant in Manchester. They were all buried here. Robert (the father of Sir James Kay-Shuttleworth), also a First Trustee and a Manchester merchant, was buried at Bamford chapel in 1834. (Page 90)

These facts were gleaned from 'The History of Park Congregational Church, Ramsbottom' By The Rev. W. E. Harding, B.A., B.D. Minister from 1925.

MEMORIAL TO ROBERT KAY, (1768-1834)
FATHER OF
SIR JAMES PHILLIPS KAY-SHUTTLEWORTH (1804-1877)
IN BAMFORD CHAPEL, ROCHDALE 1834

THE MEMORIAL READS:-

BENEATH THIS TABLET
ARE INTERRED
THE REMAINS OF
ROBERT KAY
OF BROOKSHAW NEAR BURY
WHO DIED 25TH APRIL 1834
AGED 65 YEARS.

Robert Kay was the grandfather of the 1st. Lord Shuttleworth.

In 1842 Dr. James Phillips Kay of Bamford, Rochdale married Janet Shuttleworth of Gawthorpe. James' father was Robert Kay. Robert was a manufacturer in Bamford, which is situated between Bury and Rochdale, Lancashire. He was largely instrumental in the building of Bamford Chapel in 1801. He died of heart failure at Brookshaw, Bury ... 'and at the request of his family a place of sepulchre was granted him in that pew where he used to sit and listen to the gospel inside the chapel.'... 'He is the only person to be buried inside the chapel.'...
On the death of Robert in 1834 aged 65, James assumed the mantle of his father as head of the family.
(Quotations courtesy of the Rev. David Wiseman from his book 'History of Bamford Chapel.')

PAGE 90

THE BAMFORD HOME OF
ROBERT KAY, FATHER OF
JAMES PHILLIPS KAY, from 1821 to 1830

Meadowcroft is situated at the junction of Meadowcroft Lane and Bury Road, Bamford, Rochdale. It is now called Beaumonds.

Meadowcroft

The Rev. David Wiseman, author of 'An Illustrated History of Bamford Chapel' is seen on the right of the photograph.

Robert Kay and his family lived here from 1821 to 1830. They then moved to Brookshaw House on Moorside (now Walmersley Road) in Bury, where Robert died in 1834. He was buried in Bamford Chapel. (See his Monumental Inscription on page 90).

Robert Kay was living in Rochdale at the time of his eldest son, James Phillips baptism on Feb. 20th. 1805, according to the Bamford Chapel Baptism Register. Note that the name of Robert's wife has been amended from 'Ann' to 'Hannah'.

THE ENTRY SAYS:-

'James Phillips Son of Robert & Ann / Hannah? Kay of Rochdale born
July 20th. 1804 baptised Feb. 20th. 1805 by J. T. Parsons.'

EXCERPT OF LETTER FROM SIR JAMES P. KAY- SHUTTLEWORTH
TO A MEETING OF OLD BAMFORD SUNDAY SCHOOL SCHOLARS
1867

My dear friends,

I regret that I cannot hope to avail myself of your minister's invitation to be present at the meeting of old scholars of the Bamford Sunday School. Probably few of you know that for two or three years before I went to college and while I was living with my uncle Fenton at Bamford Hall, I took a very lively interest in your school. I was a youth between 15 and 18 years old and I devoted my leisure to the organisation and management of the boys' school. ....The Sunday School was the root from which sprang our system of day schools. ..... Long before even enlightened statesmen and leaders of public opinion cared for the education of the people, the congregation had begun the work in the Sunday School. When the government first attempted to organise national education, it not only found this machinery ready to hand, but it also, after various experiments in other directions, found that the churches and congregations contained within themselves a zeal and purpose, as to public education, which existed in no civic body, not even in the Parliament itself. ..... The schools which have sprung from the root of the Sunday School, and retain both the original aim of religious training and the congregational organisation, may well be included in a national system, supported both by the general taxation and by local rates. ..... You ought not to confine your exertions to the payment of the school pence, but to make whatever sacrifice of wages or of home service is required to assure them of thorough elementary education. .....We do not make revolutions in England, but our organisations grow and spread like our oaks. .....So this school system, which has had a congregational origin will grow, change, and spread, until it is national. ....

I often think of Bamford .... in the organisation and management of which I received, forty five years ago, the first impulse to observe, enquire and ponder on the methods and discipline of schools for the people.

I am, my dear friends, your sincere well-wisher,

James P. Kay-Shuttleworth.

Taken from the 'History of Bamford Chapel' by courtesy of the Reverend David Wiseman.

MEMORIAL TO JOSEPH FENTON
(JAMES PHILLIPS KAY'S 'UNCLE FENTON' P. 92)
AND ANN (nee KAY) IN BAMFORD CHAPEL 1840

IT
READS:-

SACRED
TO THE MEMORY
OF
JOSEPH FENTON
LATE OF
BAMFORD HALL
WHO DIED
ON THE 18th. OF JUNE 1840
IN THE
76th. YEAR OF HIS AGE
———+———
ALSO OF
ANN FENTON
HIS WIFE
WHO DIED ON THE 2nd. OF MAY
1831
AGED 69 YEARS
———+———

James lived with his 'Uncle Fenton' (see letter on page 92) at Bamford Hall for three years when he was employed at his uncle's bank, 'Fenton and Roby's Bank' in Rochdale before becoming a medical student. Joseph Fenton founded Hooley Bridge, Heywood, with 160 homes with gardens around his cotton mill. His workers were reported as 'the best housed, fed, clothed and educated in Lancashire'. After Joseph's death in 1840 his son James destroyed the old Bamford Hall and built a new one. As a result of the cotton famine of 1861 and family disagreements the bank failed. Bamford Hall, Crimble Hall, Meadowcroft and their other properties, even their horses and carriages, had to be sold. The mill closed in 1863. Fentons Bank on Yorkshire St. (site of the present Yorkshire Bank) closed in 1879. Joseph's wife Ann was the elder sister of Robert Kay. (Pages 87,90,91).

*With acknowledgements to
'Some Aspects of the Life and Writings
of Sir James Phillips Kay-Shuttleworth'.
by Frank D. Emmett.*

*The New Bamford Hall
This Hall, built in the 1840s
was demolished in the 1950s*

Photograph courtesy of Rochdale Local Studies Library

KAY-SHUTTLEWORTH MEMORABILIA.

LINTEL OVER AN EARLIER DOORWAY AT
HABERGHAM INFANT SCHOOL
(NOW DEMOLISHED)

IT READ:-

GAWTHORPE   SCHOOL
18 ⛨ 40

This lintel was over the third window to the left of the attached house (as you faced it). This window was originally the school front door. It is not known if the lintel was salvaged when the school was demolished.

There was a shield between the 18 and 40 the details of which were worn away but presumably it was the original Shuttleworth shield as Janet Shuttleworth, who was responsible for the extension of the school, didn't become 'Kay-Shuttleworth' until her marriage in 1842.

INITIALS OVER THE DOOR
OF HABERGHAM SCHOOL HOUSE
(PREVIOUSLY NAMED 'GAWTHORPE SCHOOL')
1840

*Habergham Infant
School, Burnley,
March 1983,
prior to its closure.*

*Janet Shuttleworth's initials were placed over the house door of
the school that she extended on the perimeter of the Gawthorpe Estate.
This was before her marriage to James Phillips Kay in 1842.
Part of the original school name is preserved in the present front
garden of the property, it was previously built into a back wall but
this was not its position originally.*

IT STATED:-

**NATIONAL SCHOOL
ERECTED 1832**

PAGE 95

THE STREET NAMES IN PADIHAM
CONNECTED WITH THE SHUTTLEWORTH FAMILY
c1842

These streets were built on Shuttleworth land around the Parish Church in the central part of Padiham.
Shuttleworth Street was said to be one of the most attractive streets in Padiham with its ornate Victorian houses overlooking a steep bank of woodland.
Gawthorpe street has houses of unusual design, built in 1842 and reputed to have been designed by Sir Charles Barry who was the architect of the Houses of Parliament and also engaged by Sir James Kay-Shuttleworth for the restoration of Gawthorpe Hall.
Sweethome Buildings on Padiham Road Burnley are of a similar design (Page 97).

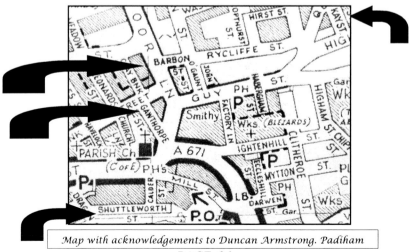

Map with acknowledgements to Duncan Armstrong. Padiham

PAGE 96

PLAQUES ON THE SWEETHOME BUILDINGS
SITUATED ON THE CORNER OF PADIHAM ROAD
AND DRYDEN STREET, BURNLEY 1856

1	2	3	4
Shuttleworth Shield	*Sweet Home Buildings*	*Erected by the I.O .of O.F. S.H.L.M.U.F.S. A.D.1856*	*Kay Shield*

These four shields are to be found on the Sweethome Buildings which are situated at the junction of Padiham Road and Dryden Street, Burnley, Lancs. just above the Stockbridge entrance to Gawthorpe.
They were erected in 1856 and are presumed to have been designed by Sir Charles Barry at the time of his involvement with the restoration of Gawthorpe Hall. The two outer shields are those of the Shuttleworth and the Kay families. The initials on shield 3 stand for 'Independent Order of Odd Fellows, Sweet Home Lodge, Manchester Unity Friendly Society.'
Similar properties are to be found on Gawthorpe Street by the Parish Church in Padiham. (Page 96).

Sweethome Buildings

*INFLUENCE OF JAMES KAY-SHUTTLEWORTH
ON GAWTHORPE.
INITIALS CARVED INTO THE STONEWORK
OF THE FIREPLACE IN THE GREAT HALL AT GAWTHORPE 1850*

*The indistinct initials of Sir James Kay-Shuttleworth and his wife,
the Shuttleworth heiress, Janet, can be seen engraved in the
stonework of the fireplace in the Great Hall.*

*The initials were placed there during the refurbishment of the hall
in the early 1850s shortly before Janet left James and went to live
on the Continent. She did not see the completed refurbishment by
Sir Charles Barry.*

 *Similar initials are to be found
in a more prominent position
above the kitchen range in the
basement.*

PAGE 98

INFLUENCE OF JAMES KAY-SHUTTLEWORTH ON GAWTHORPE.
INITIALS AND KAY MOTTO IN GAWTHORPE HALL 1850

K S on the Front Door Observation Grill

K S embossed on the Great Hall Ceiling

Obscure Initials on the Entrance Hall Fireplace

Kay Motto over the Entrance Door
'KYND KYNN KNAWNE KEPE'
—Kind Friends Know and Keep—

PAGE 99

INFLUENCE OF JAMES KAY-SHUTTLEWORTH
ON GAWTHORPE.
SHIELDS IN GAWTHORPE HALL 1850

This Achievement is surrounded on the overmantle by the small shields (L) of the Shuttleworth, Kay, Kay-Shuttleworth, and (R) Barton, Kirk, Clerke, and Holden families. The last four names relate to heiresses who married into the family.

Details of the arms on the large shield, crests and motto are similar to those on the hatchment to be found on Page 24. Small shield (in pretence):- Top:- Shuttleworth, Barton, Kirk. Bottom:- Clerke, Holden, Shuttleworth.

Library   *Details as on page 24.*   *Vestibule*

GRAVESTONE OF
SIR JAMES PHILLIPS KAY-SHUTTLEWORTH (1804-1877)
IN BROMPTON CEMETERY LONDON 1877

In ill health, James Phillips Kay-Shuttleworth spent the summer of 1876 on the Isle of Wight and then went to Cannes where he spent Christmas. He then proceeded to the house built by his late wife, Janet in San Remo. His health deteriorating, he came back to his London residence at 68, Cromwell Road, Kensington, for treatment. He died there on 26th. Of May 1877 and was buried in nearby Brompton Cemetery on Fulham Road.

IT READS:-

SIR JAMES PHILLIPS KAY SHUTTLEWORTH. BART.

BORN JULY 20TH. 1804. DIED MAY 26TH. 1877

THEY REST FROM THEIR LABOURS AND THEIR WORK DO FOLLOW THEM

Brompton Cemetery, London. (East Position, Compartment 5).

PAGE 101

PHILANTHROPIC WORKS
OF THE VICTORIAN SHUTTLEWORTHS

Sir James	Lady Blanche	Lord Ughtred
Kay-Shuttleworth	Shuttleworth	Shuttleworth

The Victorian Shuttleworths were noted for their philanthropic works locally as well as nationally. Some of these are shown below.

Sir James Kay-Shuttleworth.
Sir James was responsible for the erection of various drinking fountains and horse troughs in the area (see following page). He was also the first President of the Burnley Literary and Philosophical Society, a Life Governor of the Burnley Grammar School, and a mediator in the Miner's Strike as well as carrying out his duties as High Sheriff of Lancashire.

Lady Blanche Shuttleworth.
Lady Blanche founded the 'House of Help' with Mrs. John Brown. She also formed the 'District Nurses Association' in Padiham.

Lord Ughtred Shuttleworth.
The first Lord Shuttleworth founded the Cancer Research Clinic at the Victoria Hospital, Burnley. He gave scholarships to Burnley Grammar School and Padiham Technical College. Land was given for Ightenhill Park and Padiham Technical College. He also followed his father's example by erecting a fountain and drinking trough in Padiham. (see next page). These good works were in addition to his duties as Lord Lieutenant of Lancashire.

SHUTTLEWORTH FOUNTAINS AND DRINKING TROUGHS
IN THE LOCALITY OF GAWTHORPE

Fountains and drinking troughs such as the one shown above were donated by the Shuttleworth family for the use of the local population at the time of horse-drawn transport. The one above was erected in 1888 at the corner of Victoria Road and Burnley Road, Padiham, but as a result of a road widening scheme it was moved to the local park where it is used for floral displays. In Burnley there were fountains given by Sir James Kay-Shuttleworth and one was placed at the junction of Manchester Road and St. James' Street, another near the 'Culvert' on Yorkshire Street, and a third at Bridge End.

No photographs of the Burnley fountains have been found in the local archives but they were recorded in the 'Burnley Advertiser' of March 5th. 1859 on page 3:-

> THE STREET FOUNTAINS.
> These fountains, the gift of Sir J. P. K. Shuttle-
> worth to the town, having come, the Streets and
> Buildings Committee in their minutes recommended
> that one be placed near the Yorkshire Hotel, one at
> the Obelisk, St. James-street, and one at Bridge End.
> The recommendation was confirmed.

Their inscriptions were noted in the 'Burnley Express' of 22nd. March 1919 on page 8:-

> Gawthorpe drinking fountains, though quite
> out of use, may yet be seen at one or two
> points around the town, "K. S., 1859," pre-
> sented to the town when the present Lord
> Shuttleworth was about thirteen years old.

I am indebted to Mr. Ken Spencer for these press cuttings

PAGE 103

GAWTHORPE NORTH LODGE
GROVE LANE
PADIHAM, LANCS.

Gawthorpe Forest Lodge

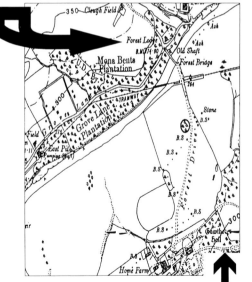

This entrance to the Gawthorpe Estate, now demolished, was situated to the north of the Hall on Grove Lane just off the Padiham/ Fence road and was used by the Shuttleworth family when inspecting their farms in the area including High Whittaker and Hollins or visiting friends and neighbours such as the Starkies of Huntroyde. The double Lodge Gate giving entrance to the drive, made of iron, painted black and gold tipped was situated to the right of the picture. This photograph, taken by Edgar Bradshaw, a Padiham photographer, was in the possession of Elizabeth Sykes, who lived there with her husband David in the 1920s. They were farmers on the Estate. David died in 1928. It was later occupied by Jim Shepherd, an estate worker whose responsibilities included the management of all the hedges.

Gawthorpe Hall

PAGE 104

GAWTHORPE SOUTH LODGES
BURNLEY ROAD, PADIHAM
AND PADIHAM ROAD, BURNLEY

Shuttleworth Shield

Stockbridge Lodge, Burnley Road, Padiham

Kay-Shuttleworth Shield

Habergham Lodge, Padiham Road, Burnley

Habergham Lodge was erected in the same period that the drive was constructed in 1862. It was used by the family when attending the church of All Saints, Habergham. It is on the Burnley side of the Estate. Stockbridge Lodge is on the Padiham side and is the drive now used as access to the Hall. It was designed by Sir Charles Barry in 1852. The above shields can be seen on both buildings.

PAGE 105

MEMENTOES GIVEN TO THE CHILDREN
OF ST. MATTHEW'S SCHOOL , PADIHAM BY
LORD & LADY SHUTTLEWORTH

In 1908, the year that Lord Ughtred Shuttleworth's eldest son and heir, Lawrence, came of age, china mugs were presented, incorporating the Baron's coronet, Shuttleworth & Kay crests and Kay motto. Some were coloured in red, others in green.

Every year each child leaving the school was given a bible. This tradition was continued by the 4th. Lord Shuttleworth until St. Matthew's school closed.

Inscription in one of the bibles:-

Inscription courtesy of the family of Alice Seabrook.

Photograph taken courtesy of Mrs. Jean Lustig. The mug, coloured in green, was given to her father Marshall S. Sutcliffe in 1908.

To celebrate Lord Ughtred's ninetieth birthday in 1934 Spode china cups and saucers were distributed. An example is displayed at Gawthorpe Hall.

LORD UGHTRED
SHUTTLEWORTH

LADY BLANCHE
SHUTTLEWORTH

TOWNELEY HALL PLAQUE TO THE

KAY-SHUTTLEWORTH BROTHERS

WHO DIED IN 1917

 *Towneley*
Hall.
Burnley.

The two sons of Lord Ughtred and Lady Blanche Shuttleworth
were killed in 1917 during the lifetime of their parents.
The next heir was the eldest grandson, Richard,
child of Lawrence, who was then aged four.
He inherited on the death of Ughtred in 1939.

A similar plaque can be seen at Gawthorpe Hall.

PAGE 107

INSCRIPTIONS UNDER THE MEMORIAL PAINTINGS TO RACHEL KAY-SHUTTLEWORTH AND HER SISTER NINA HILLS (nee K-S) IN HABERGHAM CHURCH 1967

The actual paintings could not be copied.

DEDICATED TO RACHEL:-

THE INSCRIPTION UNDER THE PAINTING FOR RACHEL READS:-

> This picture, after Raphael, and the red Altar frontal commemorate
> Rachel Beatrice Kay-Shuttleworth, M.B.E.
> third daughter of the 1st. Baron Shuttleworth of Gawthorpe
> Born 1886. Died 1967.
> 'Underneath are the Everlasting Arms'

For the life of Rachel Kay-Shuttleworth read
'Rachel Kay-Shuttleworth' by Canon G.A. Williams

BEQUEATHED BY NINA:-

THE INSCRIPTION UNDER THE PAINTING GIVEN BY NINA READS:-

> THIS FIFTEENTH CENTURY VENETIAN PICTURE
> WAS BEQUEATHED TO ALL SAINTS CHURCH,
> HABERGHAM, BY NINA, SECOND DAUGHTER OF
> THE FIRST LORD SHUTTLEWORTH, OF GAWTHORPE,
> AND WIDOW OF JUDGE EUSTACE HILLS

Nina wrote 'The Life of Sir Woodbine Parish' and was co-authoress
with her sister Angela, of the book, 'The Life of Mrs. John Brown'.

PAGE 108

THE END OF AN ERA.
DEATH OF RACHEL KAY-SHUTTLEWORTH
20th. APRIL 1967

Rachel Kay-Shuttleworth died at Gawthorpe Hall aged 81, she was the last Shuttleworth to die there.
Three years later, in 1970, Lord Charles U.J. (Tom) Shuttleworth, Rachel's nephew, gifted Gawthorpe to the National Trust.

RACHEL

The Gawthorpe Foundation   GAWTHORPE HALL
BURNLEY

Dear Michael, I want you + Frances to know that my health has broken down + that I am gently fading away. Please keep in touch with the Commander -. I am so grateful for all you have done to help -

Rachel Kay Shuttleworth
(signed on her behalf by)

This card was sent on the 16th. of April 1967, four days before her death on April 20th. It was signed on Rachel's behalf by her niece, Mrs. Janet Dorothy Young, daughter of Rachel's eldest sister Angela.
Angela also died in 1967, aged 95.
The 'Commander' referred to was Commander James Pearson, R.N., the Organising Secretary of the Gawthorpe Foundation.

SERVANTS OF

THE SHUTTLEWORTHS OF GAWTHORPE

The servants of the Shuttleworths can only be found by 'trawling' through the various documents associated with the family. Consequently the following lists are not exhaustive, they can only note the people mentioned in those accounts which have survived the ravages of time.

Family Historians who feel that they had relatives in service with the Shuttleworth family may find a mention of them here together with a note of the date and type of their employment together with the source of the information.

1580-1621   TAKEN FROM THE SHUTTLEWORTH ACCOUNTS.

Year	Name	Role
1592	HENRY WILKINSON.	BAILIFF . (FORCETT ESTATE).
1596	JAMES YATE.	BAILIFF. (GAWTHORPE ESTATE).
1601	EDWARD SHIRBURN.	STEWARD.
1608	ANTHONY WILKINSON.	STEWARD.
1609	JAMES YATE.	STEWARD.
1609	THOMAS YATES.	SERVANT.
1610	MRS. BIRCHALL.	WASHERWOMAN.
1618	JOHN POULTER.	COOK.
1621	HENRY WHITFIELD.	COOK.

1642. TAKEN FROM THE PROTESTATION OATHS
(COLONEL RICHARD SHUTTLEWORTH'S SERVANTS)

ROBERT HOULT.	JAMES WABUSLEY.
THOMAS RIDING.	THOMAS SENBY.
JOHN HILTON.	JOHN ROBERT OF CLIFTON.
RICHARD PICKUP.	GRACE POLLARD.
HENRY HALFORD.	BARNARD BESCROFT.

DURING THE PERIOD THAT THE SHUTTLEWORTHS RESIDED AT FORCETT.
1740's   ALEXANDER & RALPH NOWELL.   AGENTS FOR GAWTHORPE.

1791. TAKEN FROM ST. PETER'S PARISH CHURCH SUN DIAL (See next page).
(GAWTHORPE REPUTEDLY USED AS A FARM AT THIS PERIOD)
1791   MR.WHYMAN.   STEWARD TO ROBERT SHUTTLEWORTH.

PAGE 110

SUN DIAL ON BURNLEY PARISH CHURCH
CONSTRUCTED BY MR. WHYMAN, STEWARD OF GAWTHORPE 1791
AS MENTIONED ON THE PREVIOUS PAGE

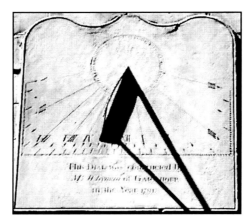

DETAIL:-

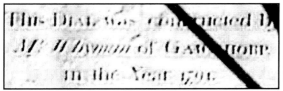

IT READS:-

This DIAL was constructed by
Mr. Whyman of GAWTHORP
In the Year 1791.

Mr. Whyman was Steward at Gawthorpe at the time of the
absentee owner, Robert Shuttleworth (P.77).
Gawthorpe fell into disrepair during this period and it was said that even the
panelled drawing room was used as a granary.

Sun Dial

St. Peter's Church
Burnley

PAGE 111

SERVANTS OF THE SHUTTLEWORTHS OF GAWTHORPE
IN THE CENSUS YEARS 1841-1891

The Shuttleworths and their house servants were not at Gawthorpe during the 1841, 1851, 1861, 1871, 1881, and 1901 census periods. In 1881 and 1901, for example, they were at their London residence.

1841. TAKEN FROM THE BURNLEY CENSUS.
(LIVING IN GAWTHORPE HALL)

SAMUEL WRIGHT.	INDEPENDENT. (N.B. MENTIONED AS 'A FAITHFUL SERVANT' IN WILL P.83)

(LIVING IN GAWTHORPE COTTAGES

NICHOLAS WADDINGTON.	GARDENER.
JAMES MERCER.	AGRICULTURAL LABOURER.
JAMES TATTERSALL.	AGRICULTURAL LABOURER.
JOHN CAMPBELL.	AGRICULTURAL LABOURER.
JOHN BALDWIN.	AGRICULTURAL LABOURER.

1851. TAKEN FROM THE BURNLEY CENSUS.
(LIVING IN GAWTHORPE HALL)

JOSEPH PATE.	AGRICULTURAL LABOURER.
THOMAS ELLIS.	AGRICULTURAL LABOURER.

(LIVING IN GAWTHORPE COTTAGES)

FREDERICK HUMPHREY GREIVES?	ARCHITECT & SURVEYOR. (ERA OF GAWTHORPE RENOVATION)
JANE INGHAM.	SERVANT.
THOMAS WOOD.	MECHANIC, FITTER.

(LIVING IN GARDENERS HOUSE)

THOMAS BIRTWELL.	GARDENER.
SARAH BIRTWELL.	————— (CLASSED AS GAWTHORPE HALL HOUSEKEEPER IN 1861)
MARY CHARLOTTE ANNE BIRTWELL.	SCHOLAR.
THOMAS JAMES BIRTWELL.	SCHOLAR.
SARAH AMELIA ELLEN BIRTWELL.	—————

1861. TAKEN FROM THE BURNLEY CENSUS.
(LIVING IN GAWTHORPE HALL)

SARAH BIRTWELL.	HOUSEKEEPER.
THOMAS BIRTWELL.	GARDENER.
CHARLOTTE BIRTWELL.	PUPIL TEACHER.
THOMAS BIRTWELL.	PUPIL TEACHER.
AMELIA BIRTWELL.	SCHOLAR.

(LIVING IN GAWTHORPE COTTAGES)

RICHARD SMITH.	FARM LABOURER.

1871. TAKEN FROM THE BURNLEY CENSUS.
(LIVING IN GAWTHORPE HALL)

SARAH BIRTWELL.	————— (CLASSED AS THE HOUSEKEEPER IN 1861)
THOMAS BIRTWELL.	GARDENER. DOMESTIC SERVANT.
SARAH A.E. BIRTWELL.	DRESSMAKER.

(LIVING IN GAWTHORPE LODGE)

GEORGE TAYLOR CAREY.	AGENT OR LAND STEWARD.

(LIVING IN GARDENERS HOUSE)

JOHN BARNES.	UNDER GARDENER.

1881. TAKEN FROM THE WESTMINSTER CENSUS.

SIR UGHTRED AND HIS FAMILY WERE AT THEIR LONDON RESIDENCE, 28 PRINCES GARDENS AT THE TIME OF THE 1881 CENSUS WITH THE FOLLOWING SERVANTS:-

JULIETTE BACHELARD.	GOVERNESS
FRANCIS WINGFIELD.	BUTLER
HARRY FORD.	FOOTMAN
BENJAMIN FOUNTAIN	FOOTMAN
JESSIE SPROTT	COOK
MARY A. KNIGHT	NURSE
HELEN E. MURPHY	LADY'S MAID
ELLEN TAYLOR	HOUSEMAID
ELLEN SMITH	HOUSEMAID
DIANA THOMPSON	KITCHENMAID
ALICE D. KEMP	NURSEMAID

(A skeleton staff, including the housekeeper, laundresses and gardeners remained at Gawthorpe but did not reside there, they lived in the locality. Alfred Ford, the Agent for the Estate, for example, was living at Cornfield House which was owned by the Estate.
(LIVING IN GAWTHORPE LODGE)

VICTOR LUCAS.	GARDENER

The Shuttleworths were 'at home' at Gawthorpe at the time of the 1891 Census.

1891. TAKEN FROM THE BURNLEY CENSUS

(SIR UGHTRED KAY SHUTTLEWORTH'S SERVANTS AT GAWTHORPE HALL)

FRANCIS WINGFIELD	BUTLER
FANNY C. MIDOL	LADY'S MAID
ADELINE MARGELLO	HOUSEMAID
MARIA MORTON	KITCHENMAID

(LIVING IN LAUNDRY COTTAGE)

JAMES PRESTON	LAUNDRY
SARAH PRESTON	LAUNDRY
RUTH A. PRESTON	LAUNDRY
FLORENCE PRESTON	LAUNDRY

(LIVING IN GAWTHORPE COTTAGES)

SILAS PRESTON	GARDENER
THOMAS ARMER	CARTER (HORSE)

(LIVING IN GARDENERS COTTAGES)

JAMES McMASTER	GARDENER
JOHN SHAW	GARDENER
GEORGE PUGH	GARDENER
HARRY WILLOUGHBY	GARDENER

JAMES McMASTER

(LIVING IN GAWTHORPE LODGE)

JOHN PEEL	WOODSMAN

This list does not include those not in residence at the time of the census, e.g.,

THEY ALSO EMPLOYED

ALFRED FORD	ESTATE AGENT	
ROBERT JEMSON	SURVEYOR	
THOMAS JEMSON	ESTATE OFFICE CLERK	
CHARLES CAMM	COACHMAN	Etc.

SERVANTS RECALLED BY ANGELA AND RACHEL KAY-SHUTTLEWORTH.

CHARLES WAREHAM.	BUTLER
MRS. MATTHEWS.	NANNY
MR. SHEPHERD.	COACHMAN
AILSIE SHEPHERD.	NURSEMAID
TOMMY WICKHAM.	ODD JOB MAN

PAGE 113

SERVANTS OF THE SHUTTLEWORTHS OF GAWTHORPE
IN THE CENSUS YEAR 1901

1901. TAKEN FROM THE WESTMINSTER CENSUS.

SIR UGHTRED AND HIS FAMILY WERE AT THEIR LONDON RESIDENCE,
28 PRINCES GARDENS AT THE TIME OF THE 1901 CENSUS
WITH THE FOLLOWING SERVANTS:-

CHARLES WAREHAM.	BUTLER
GUY J. SCOTT	FOOTMAN
SYDNEY J. CHATTERLEY	FOOTMAN
MARY JAYES	COOK
FANNY MIDOL	LADY'S MAID
JEANNE M. RIVON	NURSERY MAID
CHARLOTTE E. POVEL	NURSEMAID
ANNABELLA ALLAN	HOUSEMAID
JESSIE M. HUDDLE	HOUSEMAID
LILY WARNE	KITCHENMAID
ELLEN G. PAGE	SCULLERY MAID

(LIVING AT 51 PRINCES GATE MEWS)

CHARLES CAMM	COACHMAN

(A skeleton staff, including the caretakers, laundresses and
gardeners remained at Gawthorpe –see panel below).

1901. TAKEN FROM THE BURNLEY CENSUS
(LIVING IN GAWTHORPE HALL)

JOHN GRICE.	GARDENER.
LIZZIE GRICE.	CARETAKER.
MARY EMILY GRICE.	ASSISTANT CARETAKER.

(LAUNDRY COTTAGE)

ALICE SIMPSON.	LAUNDRESS.
ELIZABETH SIMPSON.	LAUNDRESS.
EMILY ANN BELL.	LAUNDRESS.

(CARTER'S COTTAGE)

THOMAS ARMER.	ESTATE CARTER.

(GARDENER'S COTTAGE)

SAMUEL (?) McMASTER.	GARDENER.
SAMUEL OWEN.	GARDENER.
WALTER PRIOR.	GARDENER.

(GAWTHORPE LODGE)

WILLIAM MATTHEWS.	GARDENER.
ANNIE MATTHEWS.	(NANNY?).

CORNFIELD HOUSE)

ALFRED FORD.	ESTATE AGENT.

1901. TAKEN FROM THE BARBON CENSUS
(LIVING IN BARBON MANOR)

JOSEPH KIDD.	GAMEKEEPER.
ANNIE KIDD.	CARETAKER.
MARY E. TAYLOR.	CARETAKER.

PAGE 114

GAWTHORPE SERVANTS LIVING QUARTERS

Estate Cottages.

. The Laundry block.

The Gardeners Cottages.

PAGE 115

SOME GAWTHORPE SERVANTS IN THE 20TH. CENTURY

1935 TO POST WAR

ROBERT & ELLEN
HARRISON
BUTLER &
HOUSEKEEPER

ALFRED & MRS.
PORTER.
JOINER

JOHN
HARRISON
ESTATE
WORKER

MABEL
HARRISON.
(Nee PARKER)
SERVANT

*Photographs
courtesy of John
Harrison*

<u>SOME OF THE STAFF WHO SERVED THE FAMILY DURING THIS PERIOD.</u>

FRED CROSSLEY.	AGENT. (LIVED AT STOCKBRIDGE HOUSE).
BASIL CROSSLEY.	AGENT. (").
MISS GRIMSHAW.	LADIES MAID. LATER COMPANION TO MISS RACHEL.
ROBERT HARRISON.	GARDENER. LATER BUTLER. (LIVED AT GAWTHORPE).
ELLEN HARRISON.	COOK/HOUSEKEEPER. (LIVED AT GAWTHORPE).
MABEL HARRISON.	SERVANT. ESTATE OFFICE. (LIVED IN THE ESTATE COTTAGES).
JOHN HARRISON.	ESTATE WORKER. (LIVED AT GAWTHORPE & THE ESTATE COTTAGES).
JIM SHEPHERD.	" " (LIVED AT FOREST LODGE).
DICK PINDER.	" " (LIVED IN GROVE LANE).
ALFRED PORTER.	JOINER. (LIVED AT CLOUGH FIELD HOUSE).
RICHARD BARNES.	CHAUFFEUR. (LIVED AT BARBON).

*The Staff Basement was closed in 1939
and the resident domestic staff were housed in the Estate cottages.*

SOME GAWTHORPE SERVANTS IN THE 20TH. CENTURY

1950s-1960s

MISS RIVINGTON
COMPANION

MISS WORDSWORTH
HOUSEKEEPER

MR. COPEMAN	MRS. COPEMAN	PETER LEWIS
ESTATE	HOUSEHOLD	GARDENER

Miss Rivington and Miss Wordsworth lived in the Hall.
Mr. and Mrs. Copeman lived in the Estate block in the cottage next to the
stables. Peter Lewis lived locally.

In 1970 ownership of Gawthorpe was transferred to the National Trust

KAY-SHUTTLEWORTH INSCRIPTIONS
WERE TO BE FOUND ON VARIOUS LOCAL FARMS

The initials on the downspout of
Broadhead Moor Farm,
Crown Point Road, off
Manchester Road, Burnley reads:-

18 K.S. 82

The initials of
Kay-Shuttleworth in 1882

This is one example of the types of inscriptions which were to be found on buildings owned by the Shuttleworths. A number of these buildings are now demolished. For example, Lower Holes farm, demolished in 1965 to make way for the Parklands Housing Estate, Burnley, had the inscription 'JS 1841' for Janet Shuttleworth, (as recalled by Local Historian Ken Spencer).

SOME LOCAL SHUTTLEWORTH FARMS DURING THE ERA OF THE SECOND WORLD WAR.
As remembered by Mr. John Harrison, a Gawthorpe Estate employee.

NAME	POSITION	FARMER	
		1939	1945
BROADHEAD FARM	CROWN POINT ROAD, BURNLEY	MR. ATKINSON	MR. A. CROSS
BROOKFOOT FARM	NORTHTOWN , PADIHAM		MR. WHITTAKER
BULLIONS CLOSE FARM	PARK LANE , BURNLEY		MR. E. DEAN
COPTHURST FARM	HIGHAM	MR. SEEDALL	MR. J.WILKINSON
CORNFIELD FARM	IGHTENHILL, BURNLEY		MR.W. BRIERLEY
HIGH HOUSE FARM	HIGHAM ROAD		MR. W. TODD
HIGH WHITTAKER FARM	NORTHTOWN, PADIHAM		MR. W. PHILLIPSON
HOLLIN CROSS FARM	CROWN POINT , BURNLEY		MR. N. SMITH
HOLLINS FARM	PARK LANE , BURNLEY	MR. BALMER	MR.R. WRIGHT
HOME FARM	GAWTHORPE	MR.A. CROSS	LORD SHUTTLEWORTH
HUNTERS HOME FARM	NORTHTOWN , PADIHAM	MR. BARON	MR. R. PHILLIPSON
HUNTERS OAK FARM	PARK LANE, BURNLEY		MR. W. SMITH
IGHTENHILL FARM	PARK LANE , BURNLEY		MR. R. SMITH
LITTLE TOMS FARM	HARLE SYKE		MR. HARTLEY
LOWER CLOSE FARM	PADIHAM ROAD	MR. G. COLLINGE	MR. J. ATKINSON
LOWER HOLES FARM	MANCHESTER ROAD , BURNLEY		MR. J. COLLINGE
NORTHWOOD FARM	HIGHAM ROAD		MR. J. TODD
OLD JEREMY'S FARM	HIGHAM ROAD		MR. WEBSTER
OLD MOSS FARM	HIGHAM ROAD	MR. J. WILKINSON	MR. G. HARGREAVES
RUMLEYS FARM	MANCHESTER ROAD, BURNLEY		MR. E. COLLINGE
SCHOLE BANK FARM	PADIHAM		MR. D. WHITTAKER
TOP O' THE CLOSE FARM	IGHTENHILL, BURNLEY	MR. SHACKLETON	MR. S. STRINGMAN
WELLFIELD FARM	PARK LANE, BURNLEY		MR. T. WHITTAKER
WEST CLOSE FARM	HIGHAM		MR. HODSON

PAGE 118

SHUTTLEWORTH FARMS IN THE HIGHAM AREA

IN THE ERA AFTER THE SECOND WORLD WAR

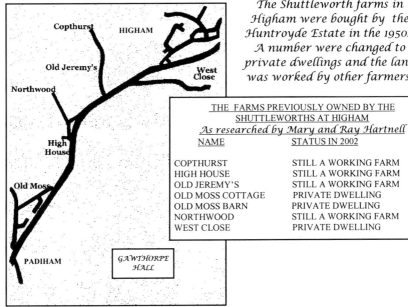

The Shuttleworth farms in Higham were bought by the Huntroyde Estate in the 1950s. A number were changed to private dwellings and the land was worked by other farmers.

THE FARMS PREVIOUSLY OWNED BY THE
SHUTTLEWORTHS AT HIGHAM
As researched by Mary and Ray Hartnell

NAME	STATUS IN 2002
COPTHURST	STILL A WORKING FARM
HIGH HOUSE	STILL A WORKING FARM
OLD JEREMY'S	STILL A WORKING FARM
OLD MOSS COTTAGE	PRIVATE DWELLING
OLD MOSS BARN	PRIVATE DWELLING
NORTHWOOD	STILL A WORKING FARM
WEST CLOSE	PRIVATE DWELLING

Map courtesy of John Benson.

The initials over the porch of Old Jeremy's farm Higham read:-

18
U.K.S.
86

The initials of Sir Ughtred Kay-Shuttleworth in 1886

Photograph courtesy of Mary and Ray Hartnell of Higham,
By permission of the Huntroyde Estate.

PAGE 119

BURIAL PLACES OF THE SHUTTLEWORTHS

HUSBAND'S NAME	DIED	BURIAL PLACE
SIR RICHARD	1599	BOLTON, LANCASHIRE?
REVEREND LAWRENCE	1608	WHICHFORD, WARWICKSHIRE.
THOMAS	1593	BOLTON, LANCASHIRE.
COLONEL RICHARD	1669	PADIHAM, LANCASHIRE.
COLONEL RICHARD JUNIOR	1648	PADIHAM, LANCASHIRE.
RICHARD OF FORCETT	1681	FORCETT, N. YORKSHIRE.
SIR RICHARD 11	1687	PADIHAM, LANCASHIRE.
READY MONEY DICK	1749	FORCETT, N. YORKSHIRE.
JAMES	1773	FORCETT, N. YORKSHIRE.
ROBERT	1816	ORSETT, ESSEX.
ROBERT	1818	PADIHAM, LANCASHIRE.
JAMES KAY-SHUTTLEWORTH	1877	BROMPTON CEMETERY, LONDON.
UGHTRED 1ST LORD.	1939	BARBON, CUMBRIA.
LAWRENCE UGHTRED	1917	VILLIERS WAR CEMETERY, FRANCE.
EDWARD JAMES	1917	BARBON, CUMBRIA.
RICHARD 2ND LORD.	1940	RUNNYMEAD (MEMORIAL).
RONALD 3RD. LORD.	1942	TABARKA WAR CEMETERY TUNISIA.
CHARLES 4TH. LORD.	1975	BARBON, CUMBRIA.

OF GAWTHORPE AND THEIR WIVES

WIFE'S NAME	DIED	BURIAL PLACE
MARGERY late BARTON nee LEGH (OR MARGARET)	1592	WINWICK, CHESHIRE.
UNMARRIED	—	
ANNE nee LEVER later UNDERHILL	1637	FORCETT, NORTH YORKSHIRE.
FLEETWOOD nee BARTON	1664	PADIHAM, LANCASHIRE.
JANE nee KIRKE		
MARGARET nee TEMPEST	1683	FORCETT, NORTH YORKSHIRE.
CATHERINE nee CLERKE	1727	PADIHAM, LANCASHIRE.
EMMA nee TEMPEST	1725	FORCETT, NORTH YORKSHIRE.
MARY nee HOLDEN	1791	
ANN nee DESAGULIERS	1801	
JANET nee MARJORIBANKS	1855	WALTON CHURCH.
JANET (HEIRESS) nee SHUTTLEWORTH	1872	SODEN. GERMANY.
BLANCHE nee PARISH	1924	BARBON, CUMBRIA.
SELINA nee BRIDGEMAN	1982	
SIBELL nee ADEANE later LYTTLETON & FULFORD	1980	BARBON, CUMBRIA.
UNMARRIED	—	
UNMARRIED	—	
ANNE ELIZABETH nee PHILLIPS	1991	BARBON, CUMBRIA.

-POSTSCRIPT-
LORD SHUTTLEWORTH
NOW RESIDES AT LECK HALL

Leck
Hall

Photograph
courtesy of
Lord
Shuttleworth

The village of Leck is in Lancashire and is situated just to the
east of the A65 at Cowan Bridge south of Kirkby Lonsdale.
Leck Hall was built on the Leck estate in 1801 by John Webb for
Robert Welsh, a Liverpool merchant, and altered in the 1830's.
The Fourth Lord Shuttleworth bought Leck Hall in 1952, being
adjacent to his estate at Barbon, and took up residence there
from Gawthorpe Hall in 1953, restoring and embellishing it.
Gawthorpe was gifted to the National Trust in 1970.
The Fifth Lord Shuttleworth, the present Lord Lieutenant of
Lancashire, still resides at Leck with his family. He was
married at St. Peter's Church, Leck and his three children
were baptised there (page 5).

With acknowledgements
to 'Leck Hall, Lancashire'
by John Martin Robinson.

St. Peter's,
Leck

PAGE 122

INDEXES

ALPHABETICAL INDEX OF THE
MISCELLANEOUS INSCRIPTIONS AND REFERENCES

PAGE

SHUTTLEWORTH WILLS

SHUTTLEWORTH AND KAY FAMILY TREES

INDEX —PEOPLE

PAGE

INDEX—PEOPLE

PAGE

PAGE 125

INDEX —PEOPLE

PAGE

PAGE 126

INDEX —PEOPLE

PAGE

PAGE 127

INDEX —PEOPLE

PAGE

INDEX—PEOPLE

PAGE

MYSTERIES AND MEMORABILIA OF GAWTHORPE AND THE SHUTTLEWORTHS

INDEX — PLACES
PAGE

INDEX — PLACES

PAGE

INDEX — PLACES
PAGE

Shuttleworth Family Tree

Richard Shuttleworth (of Forcet) – 1644 - 81. = Margaret – dau. of John Tempest d. 1683   m. 1664

Sir Richard Shuttleworth 1666 - 87. = Catherine – dau. and heiress of Henry Clarke – Magdalen College – Oxon 1667 - 1728   m. 1682

Richard Shuttleworth 1683 - 1749 – (Ready Money Dick) = Emma – dau. of William Tempest – d. 1725   m. 1707

Richard – 1708 - c1730. d. unmarried in Naples.

James Shuttleworth 1714 - 73. = Mary – dau. and heiress of Robert Holden of Aston Hall – Derbyshire – 1718 - 91.   m. 1742

Robert Shuttleworth c 1745 - 1816. = Anne – dau. of Gen. Thomas Desgauliers d. 1801.   m. 1776

James Shuttleworth of Barton – d. 1846. (inherited Barton)

Robert Shuttleworth – c 1784 - 1818. "The People's Magistrate" – inherited Gawthorpe = Janet – dau. of Sir John Marjoribanks d. 1855   m. 1816

Janet Shuttleworth heiress – 1817 - 72. = Sir James Kay-Shuttleworth – 1st Baronet 1849 1804 - 77 (became Kay-Shuttleworth 1842)   m. 1842

Sir Ughtred Kay-Shuttleworth – 2nd Bt. (1844 - 1939) – created Lord Shuttleworth 1902. = Blanche – dau. of Sir Woodbine Parish 1851 - 1924   m. 1871

Angela 1872 - 1967

Nina 1879 - 1948

Rachel 1886 - 1967

Flying Officer Richard, 2nd Lord – 1913 - 40 – Killed in action

Capt. Lawrence 1887 - 1917 Killed in action = Selina – dau. of Gen. Francis Bridgeman   m. 1913

Capt. Ronald, 3rd Lord 1917 - 42 – Killed in action

Capt. Edward – 1890 - 1917 Killed on military service

Catherine 1894 - 1963

Major Charles 4th Lord – 1917 - 75 Gave Gawthorpe to Nat. Trust, 1970 = Sibell – dau. of Charles Adeane of Cambridge.   m. 1914 | Anne – dau. of Col. Phillips   m. 1947

Charles – 5th Lord b. 1948 = Anne – dau. of James Whatman   m. 1975

PEDIGREE OF THE GAWTHORPE SHUTTLEWORTHS.

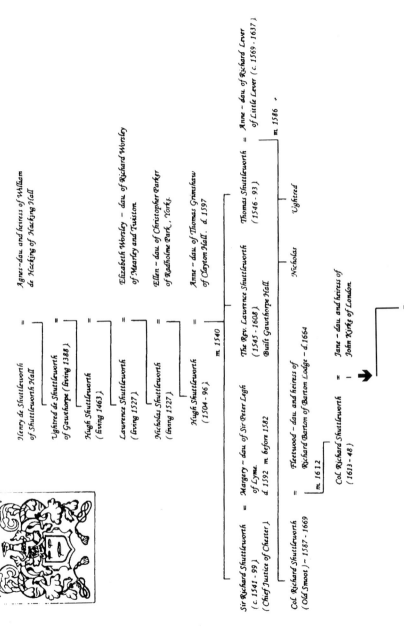

Henry de Shuttleworth of Shuttleworth Hall = Agnes – dau and heiress of William de Hacking of Hacking Hall

Ughtred de Shuttleworth of Gawthorpe (living 1388) =

Hugh Shuttleworth (living 1463) =

Lawrence Shuttleworth (living 1527) = Elizabeth Worsley – dau of Richard Worsley of Wearley and Twiston.

Nicholas Shuttleworth (living 1527) = Ellen – dau of Christopher Parker of Radholme Park., Yorks.

Hugh Shuttleworth (1504 – 96) = Anne – dau of Thomas Grimshaw of Clayton Hall. d. 1597

m. 1540

The Rev. Lawrence Shuttleworth (1545 – 1608) Built Gawthorpe Hall

Thomas Shuttleworth (1546 – 93) = Anne – dau of Richard Lever of Little Lever (c. 1569 - 1637)

m. 1586

Nicholas

Ughtred

Sir Richard Shuttleworth (c. 1541 - 99) (Chief Justice of Chester) = Margery – dau of Sir Peter Legh of Lyme. d. 1592 m. before 1582

Col. Richard Shuttleworth (Old Smoot) – 1587 - 1669 = Fleetwood – dau and heiress of Richard Barton of Barton Lodge – d.1664

m. 1612

Col. Richard Shuttleworth (1613 - 48) = Jane – dau and heiress of John Kirke of London.

INDEX OF THE MEMORIALS